A Great Teacher Is First A Great Learner

Mastering Growth, Innovation, and Impact Beyond the Classroom

Dr. Magdeline Singh

INDIA • SINGAPORE • MALAYSIA

ISBN
Paperback 979-8-89906-082-3
Hardcase 979-8-89906-083-0

Dedicated

To

My Beloved Parents – My First Teachers

Late Bernard Singh & Mrs. Florence Singh

For their enduring love, wisdom, and the invaluable lessons that have shaped my journey as both a learner and an educator.

Contents

Section I

Self-Mastery

(Developing personal growth, mindset, and well-being as a teacher)

Section II

Learner Mastery

(Understanding students, how they learn, and their evolving needs)

Contents

Section III

Teaching Mastery

(Developing core teaching strategies for modern classrooms)

Section IV

Mastery Beyond The Blackboard

*(Practical strategies for Tackling real-world classroom challenges with
effective solutions)*

Contents

Section V

Professional Mastery

(Empowering teachers with Essential skills for growth, balance, and success in teaching.)

Acknowledgment

Writing this book, *A Great Teacher Is First a Great Learner*, has been a journey of deep reflection and growth. This endeavour would not have been possible without the steadfast support, guidance, and encouragement of many individuals who have inspired and nurtured my passion for learning and teaching.

I owe my deepest gratitude to my family for nurturing my passion for teaching, a journey profoundly shaped by my late father, Bernard Singh, whose unwavering dedication to education remains my guiding light. I am equally grateful for the inspiring lives of my brothers in the field of teaching and administration, whose encouragement, expertise, and belief in this vision have been invaluable in bringing this book to life.

I express my heartfelt gratitude to Sister Eva Anju Lakra, Provincial of the Province of North East India and Nepal, and Sister Edel Rai, General Councillor of the Congregation of the Sisters of St. Joseph of Cluny, for their constant support and encouragement.

I am deeply thankful to all my animators, sisters, and well-wishers with whom I have lived and worked, whose motivation, trust, and kindness have given me strength and inspiration at every step. Their belief in me has been instrumental in shaping this work.

With profound gratitude, I acknowledge all my teachers, from my early elementary school days to my higher education and academic research journey. Each of them has played a vital role in shaping my mind and spirit, instilling in me the values of curiosity, perseverance, and lifelong learning. Their wisdom, patience, and guidance have left an indelible mark on my life, and their dedication as true mentors has been a source of inspiration throughout my academic and professional path.

A special note of gratitude to all the teachers and students I have worked with for over a decade in various schools and a college. Their passion for learning, dedication, and enthusiasm have enriched my journey as an educator and reaffirmed my belief that teaching and learning are inseparable.

To all educators, lifelong learners, and passionate readers, this book is for you. May it serve as a companion on your journey of growth and discovery. I am profoundly grateful for the countless experiences, lessons, and insights that have shaped these pages. Learning is a lifelong pursuit, and I feel truly blessed to walk this path alongside such inspiring individuals.

With immense gratitude,

– Dr. Magdeline Singh

Preface

In my family, teaching was never just a profession—it was a way of life. I grew up surrounded by educators, from my father, the first headmaster of a school in the remote village of Lingskha, Kalimpong District, West Bengal, to my two eldest brothers, who now lead government schools as headmasters. Our home was filled with conversations about classrooms, students, teachers, and the ever-evolving challenges of education. Naturally, I, too found my calling in teaching—a journey that has now spanned over a decade.

Over the years, I have realized something profound: **A great teacher is, first and foremost, a great learner.**

In a world that is constantly evolving, where new technologies, pedagogies, and student needs emerge every day, teachers can no longer rely solely on traditional methods. To truly ignite minds and shape futures, we must embrace growth, innovation, and adaptability—not just for our students but for ourselves.

This book is both a guide and a companion for every teacher who wants to thrive in the modern classroom. It is divided into five sections:

- **Section I: Self-Mastery** explores the personal growth and resilience essential for thriving as a teacher. Teaching is demanding, and before we can inspire students, we must first cultivate our own well-being, mindset, and emotional intelligence. This section delves into strategies for managing stress, maintaining a healthy work-life balance, and fostering a growth-oriented mindset to ensure sustainability and fulfilment in the profession.

- **Section II: Learner Mastery** focuses on understanding how students learn and the evolving needs of different generations. Every learner is unique. By recognizing diverse learning styles, harnessing metacognition and brain function, and understanding the impact of sleep and digital exposure, teachers can create environments that maximize student engagement and knowledge retention.

- **Section III: Teaching Mastery** highlights innovative instructional strategies that go beyond traditional methods. It underscores the importance of fostering critical thinking, integrating technology effectively, and leveraging AI as a supportive tool rather than a replacement for human connection. This section encourages teachers to reimagine their role as facilitators of deep, meaningful learning experiences.

- **Section IV: Mastery Beyond the Blackboard** addresses real-world classroom challenges and how teachers can adapt to the evolving landscape of education. From rethinking attendance and homework policies to evaluating the relevance of handwriting and dress codes, this section explores practical solutions that enhance student engagement and overall learning outcomes.

- **Section V: Professional Mastery** focuses on sustaining long-term success in the teaching profession. It provides insights into harnessing feedback, strengthening parent-teacher relationships, managing careers and finances, and preparing for a fulfilling retirement. Teaching is not just a job but a lifelong journey, and this section equips educators with the tools to thrive both professionally and personally.

Each chapter is designed to inspire, challenge, and equip teachers with practical strategies to become an educator who not only teaches but also transforms lives.

I invite you to embark on this journey with me. Whether you are a seasoned teacher, a new educator, or someone passionate about learning, this book will challenge you to see teaching as a continuous evolution. When teachers choose to grow, they create classrooms that inspire—and that is where real learning begins.

Let's embrace this journey of learning, unlearning, and relearning—together.

– Dr. Magdeline Singh

Introduction

What makes a teacher truly exceptional? While subject expertise, passion, and the ability to inspire are essential, one key truth stands above all others—you, as a teacher, are first and foremost a learner. Teaching is not just about imparting knowledge; it is about continuously growing, evolving, and adapting to the ever-changing landscape of education. When you embrace learning, you refine your craft and become a source of inspiration for your students.

In today's fast-paced world, where technology, neuroscience, and student expectations are rapidly transforming education, your role as a teacher extends beyond traditional boundaries. Classrooms are no longer static spaces with rigid lesson plans; they are dynamic environments that require you to be flexible, innovative, and open to new methods. The best teachers are those who see learning as a lifelong journey—one that shapes both their professional expertise and personal growth.

This book, **A Great Teacher Is First a Great Learner: Mastering Growth, Innovation, and Impact Beyond the Classroom**, is your guide to embracing your own learning journey. It is designed to empower you—whether you are just starting your career or have been teaching for decades—to master the art of teaching, innovate in your approach, and create a lasting impact beyond the classroom.

Before you can guide others effectively, you must first cultivate self-awareness, resilience, and well-being. Your teaching mastery begins with a growth mindset, emotional intelligence, and a healthy work-life balance. Since teaching demands both intellectual and emotional labour, nurturing your personal growth is essential for your long-term success and fulfilment.

However, being an effective teacher is not just about your personal growth—it also requires a deep understanding of your students. Today's learners are vastly different from those of previous generations. From understanding the cognitive processes behind learning to exploring the role of sleep, metacognition, and generational differences, you must tailor your teaching to meet diverse student needs.

Beyond understanding your students, your influence extends further—you are shaping critical thinkers and problem-solvers. This book invites you to adopt innovative teaching strategies, integrate technology, and explore the impact of artificial intelligence in education. As education evolves, your ability to embrace change will define your effectiveness in both physical and virtual classrooms.

Yet, teaching is not without challenges. Attendance issues, homework debates, the role of handwriting in a digital world, and even the significance of school uniforms—these are all part of the broader conversation on education. As an educator, you have the power to rethink traditional practices and explore practical solutions to everyday classroom challenges.

Teaching is not just a job—it's a lifelong mission. To sustain your passion and effectiveness, you must also develop essential skills beyond the classroom, such as giving impactful feedback, refining your communication, managing your career, and planning for financial security. By investing in these skills, you will build a fulfilling and sustainable teaching career that extends well beyond your years in the classroom.

Every page of this book is meant to inspire you to expand your understanding of a teacher's role in your personal and professional life.

Whether you are discovering your path as a new teacher or seeking fresh inspiration as a seasoned educator, this book serves as your roadmap to mastering growth, innovation, and impact in teaching.

Ultimately, teaching is a journey of discovery—for both you and your students. When you embrace lifelong learning, you not only elevate your own effectiveness but also ignite a passion for learning in those you teach. This book is here to remind you that learning is not just something you teach—it's something you live.

Your growth as a teacher, your ability to innovate, and your impact on future generations begin here. Teaching is not just about what you know—it's about how you grow. Your legacy as a teacher isn't just in the lessons you deliver but in the lives you transform.

Let your journey begin!

Section -I
Self-Mastery

(Developing personal growth, mindset, and well-being as a teacher)

Self-Mastery

A great teacher first masters the art of self-growth, for only those who ignite their own light can truly illuminate the path for others.

Have you ever wondered what truly defines a great teacher? Subject expertise? Years of experience? While these qualities matter, the heart of impactful teaching lies in something deeper—**Self-Mastery**. Before you can inspire, lead, or transform the lives of your students, you must first learn to master yourself.

Self-mastery is about developing the inner strength, resilience, and awareness needed to navigate the challenges of teaching. It means regulating emotions when faced with difficult situations, adapting to the ever-changing needs of students, and staying motivated even when the journey gets tough. Like a sculptor refining a masterpiece, you must continuously shape your mindset, habits, and emotional intelligence to become the best version of yourself. The way you respond to stress, embrace change, and nurture your own growth sets the tone for your classroom. When you lead with authenticity and confidence, your students don't just learn from you—they are inspired by you.

This section is designed to awaken your inner teacher—the part of you that goes beyond textbooks and lesson plans. You will explore the power of a growth mindset, learning how challenges can be stepping stones to success. You'll uncover the impact of emotional intelligence, helping you forge deeper connections with students and colleagues.

Finally, you'll discover strategies to achieve work-life balance, ensuring that your passion for teaching remains strong without leading to burnout.

Mastering yourself is the key to mastering the art of teaching. As you read on, embrace this journey of self-discovery—because when you invest in yourself, you create a ripple effect that transforms the lives of those you teach.

Chapter 1
Awakening Your Inner Teacher

The greatest teacher already resides within you—awaken it, nurture it, and let it guide you to inspire others.

Dear Teacher,

Before you shape the minds of others, have you truly shaped your own? Teaching is not a mere profession; it is a calling—one that demands both an inner awakening and an unshakable sense of purpose. Is teaching truly your calling, or has it become a compromise? If you were not a teacher, what would you be? Would that alternative path align more with your passions and values? Have you settled for this role, or have you truly embraced it?

These are difficult questions, but the best teachers are those who dare to ask them, knowing that self-deception serves neither them nor their students.

The classroom is not just a space of instruction; it is a mirror, reflecting your beliefs, limitations, and potential. Every lesson you teach and every student you encounter reveals something about who you are. Are you teaching from a place of deep conviction, or are you simply following a script? Do you believe in the transformative power of education, or is this a profession you have resigned yourself to? If teaching does not ignite something within you, how can you expect it to ignite something in your students? A teacher who lacks passion cannot inspire. A teacher who does not believe in the importance of their role cannot cultivate belief in others.

Every teacher brings a unique strength—perhaps an ability to make knowledge come alive, to nurture confidence in the hesitant, or to awaken curiosity in the indifferent. But recognizing your strengths is not enough. Have you honed them? Have you pushed beyond comfort to become the teacher you are truly capable of being? Or have you fallen into complacency, allowing routine to replace innovation, and obligation to replace passion? The best teachers are those who refuse to be stagnant. They are the ones who embrace discomfort, who remain restless in their pursuit of growth, and who acknowledge that even years of experience do not make them immune to blind spots and biases.

This journey will test you. There will be days when you question your impact, when the weight of responsibility feels too heavy, and when frustration overshadows fulfilment. Some days, the effort will seem invisible, the progress imperceptible. But in these very moments, the essence of a true teacher is revealed. Teaching is not about avoiding challenges—it is about leaning into them, transforming struggles into wisdom, and using setbacks as stepping stones toward deeper understanding. Resilience in education is not endurance alone; it is the refusal to allow hardship to dull your passion or lower your expectations.

Awakening the teacher within is not a single revelation—it is a lifelong process. It demands daily introspection, a commitment to refining your craft, and the courage to unlearn outdated habits. It requires humility to accept that no teacher is ever complete, and that growth is not optional but essential. The teachers who leave lasting legacies are those who never stop evolving, who remain students at heart, and who continue questioning, experimenting, and reimagining what education can be.

So, ask yourself: Is teaching truly your calling, or is it merely a role you have filled? If this profession does not challenge, fulfil, and transform you, then perhaps the greater act of courage is not in staying—but in stepping away. However, if you find, in the depths of reflection, that teaching is where you are meant to be, then rise to meet it with everything you have. Commit to it fully. Not just in knowledge but in spirit. Not just in instruction but in inspiration. Teaching is not just what you do—it is who you choose to become.

So, awake the teacher in you and celebrate the teacher within—the one who is ever-growing, ever-learning, and ever-inspiring. The world needs teachers like you. The world needs 'unfinished' teachers—because only those who see themselves as a work in progress will continue to strive for greatness.

Awaken the Teacher in You

Before you shape young minds each day,
Pause—reflect—what lights your way?
Is teaching just a path you tread,
Or does it stir your soul instead?

The classroom is a mirror bright,
Revealing doubts, unveiling light.
Do you teach with heart aflame,
Or simply wear the teacher's name?

Strengths you hold—have you refined?
Or has routine left them confined?
Passion fades when left untamed,
Rise again—be bold, be brave!

A teacher's path is never done,

It bends, it shifts, it's never one.

The best will question, break, and mend,

And find new ways to re-ascend.

25

So ask yourself—does teaching call?

Does it lift you, soul and all?

For the world needs teachers strong and true

And that, dear teacher, starts with you.

Chapter 2
The Hidden Cost of Teaching

Teaching is a gift that comes with unseen costs—only by balancing the body, mind, and spirit can a teacher continue to give without running empty.

Teaching is undeniably rewarding, yet it demands immense energy—emotionally, physically, and mentally. You dedicate hours to preparing lessons, grading assignments, and nurturing students' growth. But have you ever stopped to ask: *At what cost?* How often do you prioritize yourself amidst the endless demands of the profession? Burnout is not just a possibility; it is a reality for many teachers who struggle to balance their well-being with their professional responsibilities.

To be an effective teacher, you must first nurture yourself. Your well-being shapes your ability to inspire, engage, and lead with purpose. When you neglect self-care, the passion that once fuelled your journey begins to fade, leaving you exhausted and disconnected. Pause for a moment and ask yourself—Am I merely surviving, or am I truly thriving?

Do you know you are more than your title? Oh yes! You are more than your title; you are more than a teacher. You are a person with dreams, ambitions, and a life beyond the classroom. Have you unknowingly reduced your identity to your profession? Being passionate about teaching does not mean losing yourself in it. Recognizing and nurturing your whole self does not make you less dedicated—it makes you stronger, more fulfilled, and more effective.

True well-being is not just about avoiding exhaustion; it is about creating a life that nourishes your body, mind, and spirit. A balanced teacher is not only someone who excels in the classroom but also someone who thrives in life. Your students deserve the best version of you—but before anyone else, you deserve the best version of yourself.

So, ask yourself: What steps am I taking to reclaim my balance? Take time to reflect on your well-being—physically, mentally, and spiritually. Pause, assess where you stand, and take meaningful steps toward a healthier, more fulfilled version of yourself. Because when you flourish, so does your teaching.

Physical Well-Being

Teaching is a physically demanding profession that requires sustained energy and endurance. The long hours of standing, constant movement, and high-energy interactions can take a toll on your body. Many teachers often neglect their physical well-being, pushing themselves beyond their limits in an effort to meet professional expectations. However, when your body is exhausted, your mind follows, leading to decreased focus, increased stress, and eventual burnout. Maintaining your physical health is not a luxury but a necessity. A well-cared-for body ensures that you remain not only present but also fully engaged and effective in the classroom.

Respect Your Sleep Cycle: Sleep is the foundation of overall well-being, yet many teachers sacrifice it in the name of productivity. Chronic sleep deprivation does more than just cause tiredness—it significantly impairs cognitive functions, weakens memory retention, and affects emotional stability. A lack of sleep can lead to irritability, poor decision-making, and decreased patience, all of which negatively impact your interactions with students and colleagues. The irony is that while you emphasize the importance of proper rest to students, you often fail to apply the same principle to yourself. Prioritizing at least seven hours of quality sleep is essential. Establishing a consistent bedtime routine, reducing screen time before bed, and creating a relaxing sleep environment can enhance sleep quality. When you are well-rested, you are not just more productive but also more capable of handling the challenges that come with the profession.

Move Your Body Regularly: Although teaching involves a great deal of movement, it is important to engage in intentional physical activity beyond the natural motions of the classroom. Prolonged periods of standing without proper posture, as well as hours of grading papers while sitting, can lead to physical strain. Regular movement helps in maintaining flexibility, improving circulation, and preventing fatigue. Simple habits, such as stretching between classes, taking a short walk during breaks, or incorporating light exercises at home, can make a significant difference. Even minor adjustments, like choosing to stand while giving a lecture instead of sitting or taking the stairs instead of the elevator, contribute to your long-term physical well-being. Movement is not just about exercise; it is about sustaining your energy levels and ensuring that your body remains strong enough to support the demands of teaching.

Nourish Your Body Properly: Nutrition plays a crucial role in your daily performance, yet it is one of the most overlooked aspects of well-being. The pressures of a packed schedule often lead you to rely on caffeine, processed snacks, or skipping meals altogether. However, poor nutrition results in energy crashes, reduced concentration, and weakened immunity. Coffee, while a useful stimulant, cannot replace a well-balanced meal. Skipping breakfast or consuming sugary, processed foods leads to fluctuations in blood sugar levels, causing mood swings and decreased stamina throughout the day. A well-nourished body enhances cognitive function, improves mood, and increases endurance. Make a conscious effort to eat nutrient-rich meals, stay hydrated, and practice mindful eating. Prioritizing whole foods, such as fruits, vegetables, proteins, and whole grains, fuels your body with the energy required for sustained performance in the classroom. Hydration is equally important, as dehydration can lead to fatigue and headaches. Carry a water bottle and take small hydration breaks throughout the day to maintain your energy levels.

Listen to Your Body's Signals: Pain and fatigue are not signs of weakness—they are your body's way of signalling that something is wrong. As a teacher, you often push yourself past your physical limits, ignoring minor discomforts until they develop into serious health issues. Frequent headaches, muscle tension, and excessive tiredness are all indications that your body is under strain. Rather than dismissing these signals, take them seriously. If your body demands rest, honor it. A sick or exhausted teacher is not effective in the classroom. Allowing time for proper recovery, whether through short breaks during the day or full days of rest when necessary, ensures your long-term sustainability. Seeking medical advice when experiencing persistent health issues is also crucial. Preventive care, such as regular medical check-ups, stretching routines, and stress-relieving activities, can help you maintain overall physical well-being.

Taking care of your physical health is not just about avoiding illness; it is about sustaining your energy, enthusiasm, and endurance. A well-nourished, well-rested, and physically active teacher is better equipped to handle the daily challenges of the classroom. Prioritizing your physical well-being is not selfish—it is essential for maintaining the passion and stamina needed for a long and fulfilling teaching career. As a teacher, you serve as a role model, and by practicing self-care, you set an example for students on the importance of maintaining a balanced and healthy life.

Mental Well-Being

Your mental health is often the first to suffer under the weight of teaching responsibilities, as the constant pressure to manage lesson plans, discipline students, and meet administrative expectations can be overwhelming. The exhaustion of meeting deadlines, handling classroom challenges, and fulfilling the emotional needs of students can create an invisible burden that, if left unchecked, leads to burnout. Teaching is not just a profession—it is a calling that demands emotional resilience, adaptability, and firm dedication. However, many teachers push themselves beyond their limits, believing that sacrificing personal well-being is part of the job, when in reality, an overworked and emotionally drained teacher cannot give their best to students. Prioritizing your mental well-being is not an act of selfishness but a necessity for maintaining clarity, balance, and passion in your teaching journey. By setting boundaries, practicing emotional regulation, and embracing self-compassion, you can shift from merely coping to truly thriving, ensuring that both you and your students benefit from a healthy, engaged, and fulfilled teacher.

Set boundaries with your workload: As a teacher, you are no stranger to the long hours spent planning lessons, grading assignments, and juggling countless co-curricular responsibilities. The desire to go the extra mile for your students is commendable, but overworking does not equate to effectiveness. If you constantly push beyond your limits, exhaustion and burnout will eventually follow. Know when to stop. Permit yourself to disconnect after work hours. Close the laptop, leave emails for the next day, and set clear boundaries between work and personal time. Prioritizing rest does not mean neglecting your responsibilities—it means ensuring that you are recharged enough to handle them effectively. A well-rested teacher brings clarity, patience, and creativity into the classroom, while an overworked one struggles to stay engaged.

Practice emotional regulation: Every teacher faces difficult moments—a disruptive student, an unsupportive administrator, or a lesson that does not go as planned. These challenges can feel overwhelming, especially when they pile up. However, rather than internalizing negativity, step back and assess the situation. Ask yourself: Can I control this situation? If not, can I control my reaction? Shifting your focus from what is beyond your control to what you can manage helps you maintain emotional balance. Techniques like deep breathing, mindful reflection, or simply taking a short walk between classes can help you regain perspective. By responding to challenges with a calm and collected mindset, you not only protect your well-being but also set a positive example for your students.

Avoid the trap of self-criticism: Many teachers struggle with perfectionism, constantly feeling the need to deliver flawless lessons and meet unrealistic expectations. However, no lesson will always go perfectly, and not every student will respond as expected. Perfectionism is a silent enemy—it feeds self-doubt and drains confidence. Instead of saying, "I failed at this," shift your mindset to "I am learning from this." Mistakes and setbacks are not reflections of your competence but opportunities for growth. Recognizing that teaching is a continuous learning process allows you to embrace imperfections without guilt. When you show yourself the same patience and understanding that you offer your students, you cultivate a healthier, more resilient mindset.

Seek support when needed: Teaching can sometimes feel isolating, especially when you are dealing with stress, self-doubt, or overwhelming responsibilities. However, you are not alone. Many teachers face similar challenges, and seeking support is a sign of strength, not weakness. Lean on fellow teachers, mentors, or professional counsellors when you need guidance or encouragement. Talking about your experiences, sharing frustrations, or even simply venting to a trusted colleague can relieve mental burdens and help you find solutions. A strong support system fosters resilience and reminds you that you do not have to navigate the challenges of teaching alone.

Engage in activities that recharge you: Your identity is not solely defined by your role as a teacher—you are also an individual with personal interests, passions, and needs. What brings you peace outside of teaching? Is it reading a book, listening to music, spending time in nature, or engaging in a creative hobby? Make time for activities that nourish your mind and bring you joy. Engaging in fulfilling personal activities allows you to return to the classroom with a refreshed perspective, renewed patience, and restored enthusiasm. A mentally refreshed teacher is not only more productive but also more compassionate and effective.

Your mental health is not an afterthought—it is the foundation upon which effective teaching stands. When you prioritize your well-being, you enhance your ability to support your students, adapt to challenges, and sustain long-term passion for your profession. A healthy mind fosters creativity, patience, and emotional stability, all of which are essential in creating a positive learning environment. Remember, *you cannot pour from an empty cup.* Taking care of yourself is not a distraction from your responsibilities—it is what enables you to fulfill them with energy, clarity, and purpose.

Spiritual Well-Being

Spiritual well-being is not just about faith or religion—it is about finding meaning, purpose, and connection in your journey as a teacher. Have you lost sight of why you chose this path? Do you still feel inspired by your role, or has it become just another job? The daily demands of teaching can sometimes overshadow the deeper sense of fulfilment that initially drew you to the profession. However, nurturing your spiritual well-being can help you reconnect with your purpose and rediscover the passion that makes teaching more than just a career.

Reignite your "Why": One of the most powerful ways to restore your spiritual well-being is to reignite your "why." Teaching is not merely a job—it is a calling. Think back to what first inspired you to step into the classroom. Was it the desire to shape young minds, to make a difference, or to inspire curiosity and growth? Reflect on those moments when a student's progress filled you with joy, and hold onto them as reminders of the profound impact you have. When the challenges feel overwhelming, reconnecting with these moments can reignite your passion and give you the strength to keep going.

Engage in practices that bring you peace: Incorporating daily practices that bring you peace can also help you maintain spiritual balance. Whether it is journaling, meditation, prayer, or deep breathing, find rituals that help you feel grounded. Even five minutes of stillness in the morning can set the tone for a centred, purposeful day. By creating space for reflection and mindfulness, you allow yourself to approach teaching with renewed energy and a deeper sense of fulfilment.

Connect with Like-Minded Individuals: Another essential aspect of spiritual well-being is connecting with like-minded individuals. A strong, supportive community can provide encouragement and renewal when you feel drained. Surround yourself with teachers who share your passion, engage in meaningful conversations with colleagues, or join professional networks that uplift and inspire you. These connections remind you that you are not alone in your journey and that shared experiences can bring strength and perspective.

Detach from External Validation and Look Within: Finally, detach from external validation and look within. Your worth as a teacher is not defined by student scores, administrative praise, or societal recognition. You are enough simply by being you, and your impact extends far beyond what can be measured. Find peace in knowing that the lessons you impart, the values you instil, and the inspiration you provide cannot always be quantified. When you shift your focus from external approval to internal fulfilment, you cultivate a deeper sense of spiritual well-being that sustains you through both the triumphs and challenges of teaching.

I Am My Own Ripple Effect

*Read the following text **slowly and meaningfully**. Let each word sink in as you reflect on its message. Feel the weight of your words and embrace their significance as you read.*

I am more than just a teacher—I am a guide, a mentor, a spark in the lives of my students.

I give, I uplift, I nurture.

But today, I ask myself—When do I pour that same care into me?

I deserve rest. I deserve joy. I deserve to breathe without the weight of endless expectations.

I am not just my work. I am not just my responsibilities. I am a person with dreams, with emotions, with a heart that needs just as much care as the ones I nurture every day.

I deserve to slow down. I deserve to embrace stillness. I deserve to exist beyond my to-do list.

My passion is not meant to burn me out. My dedication is not meant to drain me. My love for teaching should not come at the cost of losing myself.

I deserve to step away when I need to. I deserve to say no without guilt. I deserve to protect my peace.

Because when I am whole, I give from a place of abundance.

When I am rested, I teach with energy.

When I am fulfilled, my students feel it too. My students deserve the best version of me.

But before anyone else—I deserve me.

Chapter 3
Embracing A Growth Mindset

A teacher with a growth mindset sees not just what is but what can be—nurturing potential, embracing challenges, and transforming effort into excellence.

Teaching is not just about what you do in the classroom—it's about who you are as a learner. You encourage your students to embrace challenges, take risks, and grow from failure, but have you ever stopped to ask yourself: Do I practice what I preach?

Embracing a growth mindset means stepping beyond the familiar, pushing past self-imposed limits, and daring to grow. It's not about being perfect—it's about being better than you were yesterday. Every challenge is a lesson, every failure a stepping stone, and every effort a spark that fuels mastery. The greatest breakthroughs come when you leave your comfort zone and embrace the unknown with curiosity and resilience. So ask yourself: Are you stretching your potential or settling for what feels safe? Growth happens when you choose courage over complacency—when you dare to believe that your best is yet to come.

Think about the moments when you struggled to implement a new method or hesitated to change an old habit. Did you retreat into what was familiar, or did you push forward? Every challenge you embrace shapes you into a more dynamic educator. Your students don't just learn from your lessons—they learn from your example.

So, here's the challenge: Will you settle into the safety of routine, or will you dare to grow? It's time to disrupt old patterns, embrace uncertainty, and become the kind of teacher who lives the mindset they teach. Your growth is just as important as your students'—are you ready to take the leap?

Unmasking the Hidden Barriers to Growth

A growth mindset isn't something you stumble upon—it's a deliberate choice, a mindset you cultivate every day. But let's be honest: Shifting from a fixed to a growth mindset isn't always easy. What invisible forces keep you anchored in the familiar, stopping you from stepping into new possibilities? Let's expose the silent roadblocks that might be holding you back:

Fear of failure: Are you holding yourself back? Have you ever avoided trying a new teaching strategy because you feared it might not work? Maybe you worry about losing credibility or feeling inadequate in front of students and colleagues. But here's the truth: failure isn't a sign of incompetence; it's proof that you're pushing boundaries. What if you embraced failure as a stepping stone to mastery instead of a mark of defeat?

The comfort of routine: Familiarity feels safe, but is it also keeping you from evolving? If you find yourself relying on the same teaching methods year after year, ask yourself: are these strategies truly effective or just comfortable? Growth begins when you dare to break patterns, experiment, and explore new possibilities.

The illusion of fixed abilities: Do you truly believe in growth? You encourage your students to believe that intelligence isn't fixed, but do you hold limiting beliefs about them—or even about yourself? If you've ever thought, *Some students just aren't cut out for this subject* or *I'll never be good with technology,* pause and challenge that thought. What if the only thing standing between you and a breakthrough is the belief that change is possible?

Resistance to feedback: Feedback isn't an attack—it's a mirror. But do you welcome it, or do you brace yourself for criticism? True growth happens when you shift from defending your teaching methods to refining them. The best teachers aren't the ones who always get it right—they're the ones willing to listen, adjust, and improve.

Time and resources: Teaching is demanding, and time always feels scarce. But growth doesn't require monumental shifts overnight. It starts with small, intentional changes—reading one article, trying one new approach, or taking five minutes at the end of the day to reflect. What's one small step you can take today to move past stagnation?

Recognizing these barriers is the first step toward transformation. The real power lies in taking action—one step at a time. Growth isn't about giant leaps; it's about consistent, courageous choices. Every small effort made today brings one closer to becoming a more empowered and fulfilled teacher. Stepping beyond the comfort zone opens doors to new possibilities, greater confidence, and a deeper impact. The journey of growth begins with a single, intentional move forward.

Classroom: A Living Laboratory for Growth

Thomas Edison once said, "I have not failed. I've just found 10,000 ways that won't work." This philosophy is the heartbeat of a growth mindset in education. As a teacher, setbacks are inevitable—lessons that don't land, students who struggle, and methods that miss the mark. But each challenge is an opportunity to refine, adapt, and grow. Edison's relentless experimentation led to the lightbulb—what if teaching was approached the same way? A classroom is not just a space for instruction; it is a living laboratory where innovation, curiosity, and adaptability thrive. Yet, the comfort of predictability often holds teachers back from exploring new methods. A growth-minded teacher doesn't just encourage students to embrace challenges but actively creates conditions where struggling feels safe and failure becomes a stepping stone to success. By shifting perspective and fostering resilience, the classroom transforms into a place where both teachers and students learn, evolve, and thrive together.

Reverse the Lesson – Instead of passively receiving information, students become the teachers. Assign them a concept before formally introducing it and let them explain it in their own words. Struggling to articulate their understanding forces them to think critically, make connections, and build resilience. When they finally encounter the formal lesson, they engage with it at a deeper level because they've already wrestled with the ideas on their own.

Celebrate the 'Most Creative Mistake' of the Week – Normalize errors by making them a focal point of discussion rather than something to be ashamed of. Designate time to reflect on the most unexpected or insightful mistakes students made, and ask, "What did this mistake teach you?" This simple shift helps students see errors as stepping stones to success rather than obstacles to avoid.

Introduce the 'Failing Forward' Journal – Instead of focusing only on the final outcome of an assignment, encourage students to document their learning struggles in a journal. What challenges did they face? What didn't work? What strategies did they refine? By shifting the focus from grades to growth, students develop self-awareness, perseverance, and a deeper understanding of the learning process.

Assign Impossible Questions – Present students with problems they cannot immediately solve and observe how their problem-solving approaches evolve over time. By tracking their strategies, they learn patience, adaptability, and creative thinking. This method teaches them that intelligence isn't fixed—it grows through effort and persistence.

By breaking away from conventional teaching methods, you create an environment where mistakes are embraced, struggle is valued, and learning becomes an ongoing journey of discovery. You empower students to see education not as a race to the right answer but as a process of continuous progress and self-improvement.

Bold Challenges for Growth-Oriented Teachers

Becoming a growth-driven teacher requires more than simply encouraging students to embrace challenges—it demands a deep commitment to your own transformation. Often, the greatest barriers to growth are hidden in routine, familiarity, and long-held traditions. The classroom, while a space of learning for students, must also be a space of evolution for teachers. To truly foster a culture of growth, you must actively question your own teaching practices. Are you teaching the way you were taught, or are you adapting to the ever-changing needs of your students? When was the last time you intentionally unlearned something about teaching? Do your lessons challenge your own thinking as much as they challenge your students? Have you ever handed over control, allowing students to design an assessment or co-create a syllabus? Growth begins the moment you step outside your comfort zone and allow yourself to be a learner alongside your students. By embracing change, you not only refine your teaching approach but also reignite your passion for education.

If you want to move beyond a fixed mindset and truly embody the principles of lifelong learning, it's time to break free from predictable routines. Challenge yourself in ways that stretch your adaptability, creativity, and willingness to fail forward. Here are some bold strategies to disrupt stagnation and spark transformation:

Switch Up Your Teaching Style for a Week – If you typically rely on direct instruction, try inquiry-based learning. If you're known for structured lesson plans, experiment with student-led discussions or project-based learning. Pushing yourself to teach differently strengthens your adaptability and keeps both you and your students engaged.

Create a 'Teacher Failure Portfolio' – Keep a record of your biggest teaching missteps—lessons that flopped, strategies that didn't work, or moments where you struggled. Reflect on what went wrong, what you learned, and how you adapted. Share your insights with colleagues, modelling a mindset where mistakes are embraced as stepping stones to success.

Engage in 'Educational Cross-Training' – Challenge yourself to teach a concept from a subject outside your expertise. Whether it's integrating history into a science lesson or using storytelling in a math class, stepping into unfamiliar territory builds empathy for the learning process and encourages intellectual bravery.

Run an 'Uncomfortable Classroom Experiment' – Once a month, introduce a completely unfamiliar concept to your students without prior preparation. Navigate the learning process alongside them, demonstrating real-time problem-solving, critical thinking, and adaptability. This exercise not only builds resilience in students but also reminds you that learning is a continuous journey.

True growth doesn't come from waiting for the perfect moment— it comes from daring to take risks today. It's not just about thinking differently; it's about teaching differently. By breaking old patterns, embracing discomfort, and modelling a mindset of continuous improvement, you transform your classroom into a space where both teachers and students thrive. Growth isn't a destination—it's a way of being.

Chapter 4
Harnessing Emotional Intelligence

A teacher who harnesses emotional intelligence not only understands minds but also touches hearts, creating a classroom where learning and compassion thrive together.

Imagine stepping into a classroom where learning flows effortlessly, where students are engaged, and where challenges are met with resilience rather than resistance. What if the secret to creating such a dynamic learning environment was not just in pedagogy but in harnessing the immense power of emotions?

Teaching is not merely about delivering content—it's about emotional energy, connection, and influence. While subject mastery is essential, understanding the emotional undercurrents in a classroom is what truly transforms the learning experience. The most successful teachers are not just knowledgeable; they possess a deep awareness of their own emotions and those of their students. They recognize the silent anxieties behind a hesitant answer, the frustration masked by indifference, and the enthusiasm hidden in quiet curiosity.

Emotional intelligence in teaching is about more than just empathy—it's about actively shaping the emotional climate of the classroom. A teacher who can regulate their own emotions, respond thoughtfully to students' feelings, and create an atmosphere of psychological safety fosters not just academic success but also lifelong emotional resilience. How you handle a student's outburst, acknowledge their struggles, or celebrate their small victories can determine whether they see learning as an opportunity or a burden.

By harnessing emotional intelligence, teachers move beyond rigid instruction and create meaningful connections that inspire students to engage, persist, and take ownership of their learning. When emotions are acknowledged and understood, the classroom transforms into a place where students feel seen, heard, and empowered.

Emotions: The Invisible Curriculum

Every classroom operates on two levels: the visible—lesson plans, discussions, and assessments—and the invisible—students' emotions, anxieties, motivations, and fears. While most teachers focus on the visible, the real power lies in decoding the invisible. Students may not remember everything you teach, but they will always remember how you made them feel.

How often do you consciously leverage emotions as a tool for learning?

Emotions influence memory, attention, and decision-making more than logic does. When students feel safe, valued, and emotionally engaged, their brains open up for deeper learning and retention. However, if they feel anxious, judged, or disconnected, even the most brilliant lesson will fail to stick.

Your ability to recognize, regulate, and respond to emotions in the classroom can transform passive learners into active participants. A student struggling with self-doubt may need your encouragement rather than correction, while another overwhelmed by personal challenges may need your reassurance before tackling academic tasks. By acknowledging and validating emotions, you create an environment where your students feel safe to make mistakes, ask questions, and engage in meaningful discussions.

Building emotional intelligence in your teaching doesn't require grand gestures—it thrives in the small, everyday interactions. A warm greeting at the door, a word of encouragement after a tough lesson, or a moment of active listening can shift a student's entire perception of learning. When you model emotional awareness and resilience, you empower your students to do the same. The invisible curriculum of emotions, when harnessed effectively, transforms your classroom into a space of trust, curiosity, and limitless growth.

Think about it

A bored student disengages.

A fearful student withdraws.

An inspired student leans in.

Emotional intelligence isn't just about managing emotions—it's about fostering the right ones at the right time.

Are You Emotionally Literate?

Emotional literacy goes beyond recognizing emotions; it involves interpreting, managing, and harnessing them to create a supportive and engaging learning environment. Every interaction in your classroom is shaped by emotions, yet their significance is often overlooked. Your ability to read and regulate emotions not only strengthens your relationships with students but also enhances their overall learning experience.

Emotions Are Contagious – Use Them Wisely: Neuroscience reveals that emotions are contagious due to mirror neurons in the brain. This means your emotional state does not just affect you— it directly influences your students' motivation, engagement, and learning outcomes. When you step into the classroom with energy and enthusiasm, you ignite curiosity and attentiveness. Conversely, if you carry stress or frustration, you may unknowingly spread disengagement.

Shaping the Emotional Climate of Your Classroom: Rather than merely reacting to student emotions, you have the power to set the tone. One effective strategy is to spark curiosity through unpredictability—beginning a lesson with a mystery, contradiction, or surprising fact. Equally important is reducing anxiety by fostering a culture of controlled risk-taking. Encouraging your students to experience low-stakes failures before high-stakes assessments helps them build resilience and confidence. Your energy matters—students often mirror your enthusiasm. When you bring positivity and excitement into the classroom, you naturally enhance participation and attentiveness.

Managing Your Own Emotions as an Educator: Emotional regulation does not mean suppressing your emotions—doing so can lead to exhaustion and burnout. Instead, practice emotional transmutation—redirecting emotions into constructive actions. For instance, frustration can be transformed into curiosity by asking yourself: *What's blocking my students' motivation?* This shift in perspective allows you to adopt a problem-solving mindset rather than a reactive one. Developing personal rituals, such as deep breathing exercises or power poses before entering a challenging class, can serve as emotional anchors to reset your mindset and maintain a positive presence.

Emotions as a Tool for Learning: Emotions are not distractions—they are powerful cognitive tools that enhance learning, retention, and motivation. Emotionally engaging lessons leave a lasting impact on your students and improve their ability to recall information. One way to achieve this is through emotional priming—setting the right emotional tone before introducing a lesson. For example, when teaching historical events, you could start with a compelling story or an imaginative prompt to help your students form a deeper connection with the material. Another principle to consider is the Peak-End Rule, which suggests that students remember lessons based on emotional highs and their endings. Designing your lessons with an "aha" moment and a strong conclusion can leave a lasting impression. Additionally, curiosity can be used as an emotional activation tool. A well-placed surprise, contradiction, or dilemma engages your students emotionally, increasing intrinsic motivation and improving comprehension.

Your classroom is an emotional ecosystem, constantly responding to the signals you send. The key question is not whether you experience emotions but whether you are using them as a tool for effective teaching or allowing them to control your classroom dynamics. Future education will place greater emphasis on Emotional Intelligence (EQ) alongside traditional measures of intelligence. Adaptability, resilience, and emotional mastery will be just as important as academic knowledge. By integrating emotional literacy into your teaching practices, you prepare your students for a world that values not just cognitive skills but also emotional intelligence.

When you master emotional literacy, you don't just teach—you inspire, transform, and empower, and that is the true magic of education.

How to Read and Hack Emotional Cues

Empathy in teaching isn't just about being kind—it's about truly seeing your students, even when they're not speaking. Sometimes, the most important messages aren't in their words but in their expressions, posture, and energy. The best teachers don't just hear; they listen. They don't just observe; they understand.

Try this the next time you step into your classroom. Watch for micro-reactions—a slight frown, a hesitant pause, or a downward glance can signal confusion before a student even speaks. A quick check-in, such as *"That seemed tricky. Want me to go over it again?"*, can make all the difference. Listen beyond words; if a student says, *"I'm fine,"* while avoiding eye contact, that's your cue to dig a little deeper. Sometimes, a simple *"I'm here if you want to talk"* is all they need to feel safe and supported.

Beyond individual cues, feel the room. Walk into your classroom with awareness—does the atmosphere feel tense, restless, or heavy? Your ability to read the energy in the room allows you to pivot when needed, whether that means incorporating a brain break, offering words of encouragement, or shifting your teaching approach to better engage your students.

Teaching isn't just about delivering content—it's about creating an emotional space where students *want* to learn. The more you fine-tune your ability to read and respond to emotions, the more powerful your impact will be. And the best part? Emotional intelligence isn't an inborn talent—it's a skill you can develop every single day. Keep practicing, keep adjusting, and watch how your students—and your own teaching experience—transform.

Chapter 5
Work-Life Balance

A teacher's greatest lesson is balance—nurturing minds in the classroom while nurturing their own well-being beyond it.

Teaching is a calling, a profession that requires dedication, passion, and an unyielding commitment to your students. But let's be honest—sometimes the pressure can feel overwhelming. The never-ending lesson plans, stacks of grading, meetings that seem to stretch endlessly, and the constant need to manage classroom dynamics can drain even the most energetic and enthusiastic teachers. When your days are consumed by deadlines and responsibilities, it's easy to feel as though there's little room left for yourself. That's why finding a work-life balance isn't just important—it's vital. It's not just about surviving the demands of teaching; it's about thriving, both inside and outside the classroom.

Yet, work-life balance can feel elusive. The lines between your professional and personal life blur when school-related tasks spill into your evenings and weekends. How often do you find yourself answering emails long after school hours or spending your Sunday afternoons prepping lessons instead of recharging? While your dedication to your students is admirable, it should not come at the cost of your well-being. You deserve time to rest, to engage in activities that bring you joy, and to nurture the relationships that matter most to you. Teaching should not mean sacrificing your personal happiness—it should be a fulfilling part of a well-rounded life.

This chapter isn't just a set of instructions—it's a reminder that *you* deserve a life that is rich, meaningful, and balanced. Reclaiming your time means setting boundaries, prioritizing self-care, and allowing yourself to step away from work without guilt. Imagine leaving school with a sense of accomplishment rather than exhaustion, spending evenings engaged in hobbies you love, or simply enjoying moments of stillness without the weight of unfinished tasks on your mind.

It's time to challenge the idea that great teachers must be constantly working. You do not have to choose between being an excellent teacher and living a fulfilling personal life—you can have both. The key lies in intentional balance. By learning to manage your time, delegate when necessary, and set clear boundaries, you create a more sustainable and enjoyable teaching experience. A well-rested, emotionally fulfilled teacher is not just happier but also more effective in the classroom.

So let's explore how you can reclaim your time, find joy beyond the classroom, and embrace a healthier, more sustainable way of living. Your students deserve a teacher who is energized, inspired, and present. But more importantly, *you* deserve a life that is fulfilling, both within and beyond the walls of your classroom.

Set Realistic Expectations: You cannot do it all, all the time, and that's okay. You are not a superhuman being. One of the biggest challenges teachers face is the weight of self-imposed perfectionism. The truth is, perfection is not the goal—it's progress, balance, and well-being. You are giving your best every day, and sometimes, your best means letting go of the unrealistic standards you set for yourself. Start by setting *realistic* expectations. It's easy to feel like you need to be everything to everyone, but remember: you're human. Some days will be brilliant, and others, well, will be less than perfect. And that's okay. Letting go of the pressure to be flawless is one of the most freeing steps toward finding balance.

Prioritize What Matters: Time management is more than just organizing tasks—it's about making intentional choices that prioritize what truly matters. Think of it as curating your time rather than filling it. Start by identifying your priorities. What's urgent? What's important? What can wait? Once you know this, you can use practical strategies like to-do lists, time-blocking, or digital planners to structure your day effectively. But don't forget—*delegation* is your ally. You don't have to carry the burden alone. Whether it's leaning on a colleague for help or asking a teaching assistant to take on a task, delegating isn't a sign of weakness; it's a sign of wisdom. Ask for help when you need it—it's a smart way to free up time for yourself.

And remember, you're not a machine. *Saying no* is not just permissible; it's necessary. It's a powerful tool to protect your time and your well-being. It's okay to turn down extra responsibilities when you've already filled your plate. Guarding your time and energy is one of the most loving acts you can do for yourself.

Take Breaks: It's tempting to skip breaks, especially when the list of things to do seems endless. But here's the truth: *taking breaks is not a luxury, it's a necessity.* Whether it's a quick walk around the block, a few minutes of deep breathing, or simply stepping away from your desk for a moment of quiet, breaks help to recharge your mind and body. Your energy and creativity thrive when you allow yourself to pause. *Recharge to re-energize,* and don't wait for a long weekend to rest. Small, consistent breaks throughout the day can make a huge difference. Allow yourself time to step away, even if it's just for five minutes. That time is an investment in your well-being and in your ability to give your best to your students.

Cultivate Life Beyond the Classroom: Teaching is deeply rewarding, but it's not all there is to life. It's crucial to nurture your whole self—the person outside the classroom. Pursue hobbies, take up new activities, and invest in the things that bring you joy. Maybe it's painting, playing music, reading, or cooking—whatever it is, make sure you have something outside of teaching that fuels your soul.

And remember, you deserve to spend time doing things just for you. The more you fill your own cup, the more you can pour into your work and the people around you. Having a life beyond the classroom isn't just about relaxation—it's about maintaining the passion and energy that keep you motivated and inspired to teach.

The Power of Saying "No" and Protecting Your Relationships: As a teacher, you're driven by a deep desire to help others. But here's the truth—*you cannot pour from an empty cup.* Saying "no" isn't just about managing your workload; it's about protecting your mental and emotional health. When you say "no" to tasks that don't align with your priorities, you create space for what really matters.

Equally important is carving out time for the people who make your heart full. Family, friends, and loved ones—these connections are the support system that will carry you through the toughest days. Don't let work overshadow the moments that truly nourish you. Spending time with those who care for you and who uplift you is the best way to ensure that you are grounded and centred.

Finding Harmony, Not Perfection: The truth is, there's no "perfect" balance. Life is messy, unpredictable, and always changing. And that's okay. Achieving work-life balance isn't about finding a 50/50 split between work and life every day—it's about harmony. It's about making intentional choices, day by day, that allow both your work and your personal life to coexist in a way that feels fulfilling and sustainable. You won't always get it "right," and that's fine. What matters is that you are striving for balance, for peace, and for joy.

You are a teacher—a guide, a mentor, a source of inspiration to your students. But don't forget that you are also a person, deserving of love, rest, and happiness. By nurturing both your professional and personal life, you'll create a rhythm that supports your well-being and fuels your passion for teaching. In the end, a balanced teacher is a *better* teacher.

You Are Worth It : Work-life balance isn't a luxury, and it's not just a "nice-to-have." It's essential for your longevity, for your well-being, and for the impact you make in the classroom. By setting realistic expectations, managing your time effectively, taking breaks, and protecting your personal life, you are giving yourself the gift of sustainability. And let me tell you—*you are worth it.* The world needs teachers like you, not just in the classroom but in every part of your life. Take the time to nurture yourself, and you'll see how much more you have to give.

I Am My Own Ripple Effect

Every choice I make sends ripples into the world—I choose balance, so I teach balance.

My well-being is the stone that starts the waves; when I nurture myself, my energy flows outward, shaping the classroom, the learning, and the lives I touch. A rested teacher sparks curiosity, a joyful teacher nurtures growth, and a fulfilled teacher inspires change.

I release the need for perfection, knowing that even small ripples create meaningful impact. Saying "no" is not resistance—it is an act of wisdom, a redirection of my energy toward what truly matters. My passion for teaching does not demand my exhaustion; my light shines brightest when I am whole.

The laughter I share, the moments I cherish, and the rest I allow myself are not indulgences—they are gifts I pass on to my students. Just as a pebble shapes the water, my presence shapes the future, stronger and more radiant when I am centered.

Balance is not stillness but a steady rhythm—a dance between giving and replenishing, between effort and renewal. I embrace both the ebb and flow of life, knowing that in caring for myself, I create waves of inspiration, love, and lasting impact.

* * *

Section -II
Learner Mastery

(Understanding students, how they learn, and their evolving needs)

Learner Mastery

A true teacher sees beyond who a student is today, fostering their potential with wisdom, patience, and deep belief in who they can become.

Teaching is more than just delivering lessons—it's an exhilarating journey of discovery, growth, and transformation. As a teacher, you're not just shaping minds; you're unlocking potential. But have you ever paused to consider how your students learn best? What sparks their curiosity, fuels their motivation, and empowers them to master their own learning?

Student mastery isn't about rote memorization or high test scores—it's about cultivating deep understanding, critical thinking, and the ability to apply knowledge in meaningful ways. It's about guiding students to become independent learners who don't just absorb information but engage with it, question it, and make it their own. Imagine the shift when students take ownership of their learning— when they move from passive receivers of knowledge to active seekers of wisdom.

In this section, you'll uncover the power of metacognition, helping students think about how they think so they can develop stronger learning habits. We'll also delve into the fascinating connection between rest, brain function, and retention, challenging the outdated notion that relentless studying equals success. Ultimately, understanding these principles will be crucial in supporting the unique learning needs of Gen Z, Gen Alpha, and the generations to come.

Education is evolving at lightning speed, and so are your students. The strategies that worked a decade ago may no longer resonate, but that presents an exciting opportunity: to evolve with them. By embracing new insights into student learning, you're not just teaching—you're empowering the next generation to thrive in an ever-changing world.

Chapter 6
How Learning Happens?

Learning happens when curiosity is sparked and understanding is cultivated.

The brain is a fascinating organ that shapes how you think, learn, and respond to the world. As a teacher, understanding how different parts of the brain function can help you manage your well-being and create a supportive learning environment for your students. Effective teaching is not just about delivering content; it is about fostering an environment where students feel safe, engaged, and motivated to learn. By understanding how the brain processes information, teachers can create strategies that optimize learning and minimize stress.

The human brain consists of three main layers that influence how learning takes place: the **Reptilian Brain**, the **Mammalian Brain**, and the **Neocortex**. Each plays a distinct role in shaping student behaviour, motivation, and cognitive processing.

1. Reptilian Brain

As a teacher, you've likely seen it happen—a student freezes when called upon, shuts down when faced with a challenge, or reacts defensively to constructive feedback. These reactions aren't simply signs of disinterest or defiance; they stem from the most primitive part of the human brain—the Reptilian Brain. This part of the brain controls survival instincts, including the fight, flight, and freeze responses. When students perceive a situation as threatening—whether it's fear of failure, public embarrassment, or an overwhelming workload—their brains instinctively react, making it difficult to focus, think logically, or absorb new information. Following are the stages of Reptilian Brain in learning:

Flight - The Urge to Escape: When students feel anxious or overwhelmed, their first instinct is often to avoid the situation entirely. Perhaps you've noticed a student suddenly looking down, avoiding eye contact, or making excuses to leave the classroom when they're about to be called on. This is the flight response—their brain telling them that escape is the safest option. Without intervention, this can lead to chronic avoidance, where students disengage from learning altogether.

Fight - The Defensive Mode: If escape isn't possible, the brain may shift to a fight response—not necessarily in a physical sense, but through frustration, defiance, or resistance. You may encounter students who argue about assignments, dismiss the importance of a subject, or respond with sarcasm when challenged. This isn't always a sign of disrespect; rather, it's their brain's way of masking vulnerability with defensiveness. Recognizing this allows you to respond with patience and guidance rather than frustration.

Freeze - The Mental Block : Sometimes, stress overwhelms a student to the point where they simply shut down. Imagine a student standing in front of the class to solve a math problem. As their peers giggle, their mind suddenly goes blank. They know the answer, but they can't recall it—this is the freeze response. Their brain, overwhelmed with stress, temporarily blocks access to information, making it impossible to think clearly.

Your Role in Guiding Students Beyond Reptilian Mode

Understanding these survival instincts is key to creating a supportive learning environment where students feel safe, engaged, and empowered to take risks. Here's how you can help your students move beyond survival mode and into a mindset of learning and growth:

Create a Safe and Encouraging Classroom Culture: Your words and actions set the tone. A simple, "Take your time; I believe in you," can be the difference between a student shutting down and pushing forward. When students feel supported, their stress levels decrease, allowing them to engage more fully.

Normalize Mistakes and Growth: Many students fear failure because they associate it with humiliation. By celebrating effort over perfection and sharing stories of your own challenges, you can help them see failure as a stepping stone to success rather than something to be feared.

Encourage Collaborative Learning: Group activities and peer discussions allow students to participate without the pressure of being singled out. When students feel part of a team, they are less likely to experience a fight, flight, or freeze reaction.

Use Mindfulness and Stress-Reduction Techniques: Simple breathing exercises, short mindfulness breaks, or even a touch of humour can help reset the brain, reducing anxiety and increasing focus. Teaching students to manage stress equips them with lifelong skills that go beyond the classroom.

The Reptilian Brain isn't the enemy—it's simply wired for survival. But as a teacher, you have the power to help your students override fear-based reactions and develop confidence in their abilities. Whether it's encouraging a hesitant learner, calming an anxious student, or helping a frustrated one channel their energy productively, your approach can make all the difference.

By recognizing and addressing these instinctive responses, you empower your students to face challenges with resilience, embrace mistakes as part of learning, and develop the courage to step beyond their comfort zones. In doing so, you're not just teaching a subject—you're shaping fearless, capable learners who are ready to take on the world.

2. The Mammalian Brain

Think back to your own school days—was there a teacher who made you feel seen, heard, and valued? Chances are, that connection made all the difference in your motivation to learn. That's because the Mammalian Brain, or limbic system, isn't just about emotions; it's the foundation of trust, relationships, and engagement.

Students don't learn in isolation. Their ability to absorb, process, and retain information is deeply intertwined with how safe and supported they feel in the classroom. When emotions like fear, anxiety, or loneliness take over, learning takes a backseat. But when students feel a sense of belonging, encouragement, and emotional stability, their brains become receptive, and learning flourishes.

Imagine this: Arjun, a middle school student, walks into your class, shoulders slumped, face tense. Normally full of energy, sometimes too much of it- today, he refuses to participate. You could react with frustration—*"Arjun, stop disrupting the class and pay attention!"*—but instead, you pause. You soften your tone and say, *"Arjun, I noticed you're not yourself today. Want to talk?"*

Later, you find out he had a falling out with his best friend, and his emotions are clouding his ability to focus. In that moment, you've done more than acknowledge his feelings—you've given him a safe space, a moment of trust. This small act can be the difference between disengagement and re-engagement.

Your Role in Nurturing the Mammalian Brain

As a teacher, you are more than an instructor—you are the anchor in a student's storm. Here's how you can create an emotionally supportive environment where learning thrives:

Validate Their Feelings: A simple *"I see you. I hear you. It's okay to feel this way."* can help students process their emotions rather than be overwhelmed by them.

Give Them Space to Regulate: Not every student can instantly switch from emotional distress to academic focus. A mindful pause, a quick reflection exercise, or even just a moment to breathe can help reset their emotional state.

Create a Culture of Belonging: Structured routines, collaborative group work, and warm interactions signal to students that they are part of something bigger. A connected classroom is an engaged classroom.

The truth is, when you take the time to nurture their emotional well-being, you're not just teaching—you're empowering them to believe in themselves, trust others, and engage deeply in their own learning journey. So, the next time you notice a student struggling, remember: your words, your tone, and your presence have the power to transform not just a moment, but a mindset.

3. Neocortex Brain

Imagine a classroom where students don't just memorize facts but truly think, question, and create. A space where curiosity fuels discovery and learning becomes an adventure rather than a routine task. This is the power of the Neocortex, the most advanced part of the brain, responsible for logic, creativity, problem-solving, and critical reasoning. Unlike the primitive Reptilian Brain, which triggers survival instincts, or the Mammalian Brain, which governs emotions and relationships, the Neocortex thrives in an environment that is low-stress, engaging, and intellectually stimulating. When students feel safe and excited about learning, their brains unlock their full cognitive potential, allowing them to analyze, innovate, and connect ideas in meaningful ways.

Picture this: You're introducing Newton's Laws of Motion. You could stand in front of the class and lecture, writing formulas on the board, explaining the concepts in a linear fashion. But will your students truly understand and retain this knowledge? Or will they simply memorize it for an exam and forget it soon after?

Now, imagine a different approach. Instead of a lecture, you bring the lesson to life. You start by showing a compelling video of a footballer kicking a ball, demonstrating force and motion in action. Next, you set up a hands-on experiment using toy cars and ramps, allowing students to observe Newton's laws firsthand. Then, you ask students to predict the outcomes before testing their ideas, encouraging them to think critically and engage with the material.

What happens next? The classroom buzzes with excitement. Students are no longer passive recipients of information—they are active participants in their own learning. Their Neocortex is fully engaged, transforming what could have been a dry, forgettable lesson into an unforgettable experience. When students interact with new information in a meaningful way, they retain knowledge longer and develop a deeper understanding of the subject.

Your Role in Activating Higher-Order Thinking

As a teacher, you are not just delivering information—you are shaping the way students think, analyze, and solve problems. Your role in engaging the Neocortex is essential for moving students beyond rote memorization and fostering genuine intellectual growth. Here's how you can create an environment that encourages higher-order thinking:

Make Learning Interactive: The Neocortex thrives when students can actively engage with ideas. Hands-on experiments, storytelling, role-playing, project-based learning, and problem-solving activities make abstract concepts more tangible and memorable. When students explore topics through real-world applications, they develop critical thinking skills that last a lifetime.

Encourage Curiosity and Independent Thinking: When students ask questions, challenge ideas, and explore different perspectives, they activate the full potential of their Neocortex. Create an atmosphere where curiosity is not just welcomed but celebrated. Instead of simply providing answers, guide students toward discovering solutions on their own. Inquiry-based learning encourages students to think deeply, make connections, and develop their own insights.

Create a Relaxed, Enjoyable Atmosphere: Stress and fear shut down the Neocortex, making learning difficult. A rigid, high-pressure classroom environment can push students into survival mode, where the Reptilian Brain takes over. To truly engage their higher-order thinking, create a positive, low-stress learning space where students feel comfortable taking risks, making mistakes, and learning through exploration. A joyful, engaging classroom helps students absorb and retain knowledge more effectively.

The goal of education is not just to teach students what to think but how to think. In a world that demands creativity, adaptability, and problem-solving, fostering higher-order thinking is more important than ever. When you ignite students' natural curiosity, encourage them to analyze and question, and give them opportunities to apply their knowledge in meaningful ways, you are preparing them for success beyond the classroom. The impact of your teaching extends far beyond a single lesson. Every time you inspire a student to think critically, to question, and to explore, you are shaping future leaders, innovators, and problem-solvers. You are not just teaching a subject—you are shaping minds that will transform the world.

Teaching with the Brain in Mind

As a teacher, you are responsible for the ever-changing emotional and intellectual landscape of your students' lives. Your ability to stay calm, emotionally balanced, and curious not only influences the way you teach but also shapes how students navigate their own emotions and cognitive processes. Understanding which part of the brain is dominant in a given moment allows you to adapt your teaching strategies to meet students exactly where they are. Imagine the difference it makes when you recognize that a student's outburst isn't defiance but a stress response from the Reptilian Brain, or that disengagement isn't laziness but emotional distress rooted in the Mammalian Brain. With this awareness, you can shift your approach, guiding students from survival mode to a state of engagement and curiosity.

So, match your approach to students' needs:

✓ If a student is overwhelmed and anxious (Reptilian Brain), minimize stress by creating a safe and supportive space before introducing new content. A reassuring word or a moment of quiet can help reset their brain for learning. Remember, learning cannot take place in a state of fear or anxiety. By maintaining a calm and structured environment, you prevent the Reptilian Brain from hijacking the learning process.

✓ If a student is emotionally upset or disconnected (Mammalian Brain), focus on building a sense of connection. A simple *"I see you. I hear you. You matter"* can rekindle their motivation. Students who feel emotionally secure are more willing to take risks and engage in learning. Foster trust, empathy, and a sense of belonging to keep their Mammalian Brain in balance.

✓ If a student is engaged and ready to explore (Neocortex), provide stimulating challenges, encourage creative problem-solving, and foster deep, meaningful learning experiences. The Neocortex thrives on exploration, curiosity, and problem-solving. Design lessons that are interactive, hands-on, and thought-provoking to stimulate higher-order thinking.

Your presence sets the emotional tone of the classroom. When you model patience, resilience, and a growth mindset, students learn to regulate their own emotions and approach challenges with confidence. When students feel safe, supported, and engaged, their brains are primed for deep and lasting learning. You are not just teaching a subject—you are guiding students from frustration to understanding, from emotional distress to motivation, and from confusion to clarity. Every day, you have the power to reshape mindsets, ignite curiosity, and transform potential into achievement. Teaching is about unlocking the full capacity of the mind. And the best way to do that? Teach not just with your subject expertise but with your heart, your awareness, and your unwavering belief in your students' potential.

Chapter 7
Every Learner Matters

Every learner matters, for within each student lies a unique potential waiting to be seen, nurtured, and empowered by a teacher who believes in them.

I*magine this:* You have a student, Maya, who struggles to grasp mathematical concepts no matter how many times you explain them. During lectures, she zones out, her notebook filled with incomplete notes. You start to worry—maybe she's just not good at math. But one day, you introduce a hands-on activity using colourful blocks to demonstrate fractions. Suddenly, Maya's face lights up. She starts manipulating the blocks, experimenting with different combinations, and within minutes, she exclaims, *"Oh! Now I get it!"*

Maya wasn't struggling because she lacked intelligence—she was struggling because the teaching method didn't align with the way her brain naturally processes information. The moment you recognize her learning style and adjust your approach, she will unlock her potential.

As a teacher, you encounter students like Maya every day. Some learn best through visuals, others through discussion, reading, or hands-on activities. Understanding these differences isn't just about making your job easier—it's about empowering every student to succeed.

Each student in your classroom uniquely processes information. The VARK model—Visual, Auditory, Reading/Writing, and

Kinaesthetic—categorizes learners based on their preferred way of absorbing knowledge. Recognizing these preferences allows you to tailor your teaching, ensuring that every student remains engaged and grasps the content deeply.

You have the incredible opportunity to shape young minds by adapting your teaching methods to different learning styles. Imagine a classroom where every student feels seen, heard, and understood—where lessons come alive, and knowledge is not just taught but truly absorbed. This becomes possible when you embrace the four primary learning styles, which serve as the foundation for effective teaching and meaningful learning. By aligning your approach with how your students learn best, you create an environment where learning is not a struggle but an exciting and enriching journey. Let's explore these learning styles and discover how you can make your teaching more dynamic, impactful, and rewarding!

Visual Learners -Seeing is Understanding: As a teacher, you will have students who learn best when they can see concepts rather than just hear about them. Visual learners thrive when information is presented through images, diagrams, charts, and other visual aids. They may struggle with long verbal explanations but quickly grasp ideas when they are structured and visually organized. To support these students, you can incorporate PowerPoint presentations with relevant images, instructional videos, and colourful infographics into your lessons. Encouraging your students to create mind maps, drawings, or flowcharts will help them process and retain information more effectively. Additionally, using color-coded notes or highlighting key concepts in different colours can make complex ideas more digestible. When you recognize and adapt to the needs of visual learners, you create a more engaging and inclusive classroom where every student has the opportunity to succeed. By embracing these strategies, you empower your students to unlock their full potential and make learning a more enriching experience for everyone.

Auditory Learners -Learning Through Listening: Some students absorb information best when they hear it rather than see it or interact with it physically. These are your auditory learners—students who thrive in discussions, lectures, and verbal explanations. They have a remarkable ability to retain details when they are spoken aloud and often enjoy participating in debates, storytelling, and conversations that allow them to process ideas through sound. You may notice that these students remember information from class discussions more than from written notes, and they often prefer reading aloud or explaining concepts verbally to reinforce their understanding.

To support auditory learners in your classroom, consider incorporating more storytelling, recorded lectures, and podcasts into your lessons. These tools provide a structured way for them to absorb information through listening. Engaging them in meaningful discussions, debates, and Socratic questioning will further enhance their comprehension, as they process ideas best when they can articulate and discuss them. Additionally, encouraging students to read aloud or explain concepts to their peers can strengthen their retention and deepen their grasp of the subject matter. By embracing these strategies, you create a classroom environment where auditory learners can thrive, transforming passive listening into an active and enriching learning experience.

Reading/Writing Learners-The Power of Words: For some students, the written word is the most effective gateway to understanding. These reading/writing learners prefer to process information through text, excelling in note-taking, journaling, and written assignments. They have a natural inclination for reading and often retain knowledge best when they can engage with it through writing. Whether it's summarizing key points, creating study guides, or composing essays, these learners thrive when they can translate ideas into their own words. You may notice that they prefer textbooks over videos, enjoy making detailed notes, and are more comfortable expressing their thoughts through writing rather than speaking.

To support reading/writing learners in your classroom, provide ample opportunities for them to interact with content through written materials. Assigning essays, journaling exercises, and research projects will allow them to deepen their understanding by organizing their thoughts in written form. Encouraging them to summarize lessons in their own words helps reinforce learning and strengthens comprehension. Additionally, offering handouts, written instructions, and structured study guides will enhance their ability to absorb and recall information effectively. By incorporating these strategies, you create an environment where reading/writing learners can engage with content in a way that feels natural and empowering, ultimately leading to greater academic success.

Kinaesthetic Learners-Learning by Doing: Some students learn best not by listening or reading but by physically engaging with the material. These kinaesthetic learners thrive when they can move, touch, and experience concepts firsthand. They often struggle to sit through long lectures or passive learning experiences but excel when given opportunities to interact with their environment. Whether it's conducting experiments, participating in role-playing activities, or engaging in hands-on projects, kinaesthetic learners absorb information by doing rather than just seeing or hearing. You may notice that these students fidget during traditional lessons, prefer working with tangible materials, and remember concepts better when they can physically engage with them.

To support kinaesthetic learners in your classroom, incorporate interactive activities that encourage movement and hands-on experiences. Using experiments, simulations, and role-playing exercises can help them connect with abstract concepts in a concrete way. Movement-based learning activities, such as educational games, group exercises, or even simple physical gestures tied to lessons, can make learning more engaging and effective. Additionally, encouraging real-world problem-solving, outdoor learning, and project-based assignments allows these students to apply their knowledge in meaningful ways. By integrating these strategies, you create a dynamic learning environment where kinaesthetic learners can stay actively engaged, making education an exciting and immersive journey.

Beyond Learning Styles

As a teacher, you know that no two students learn in exactly the same way. While learning styles help you understand how students absorb information, true mastery of teaching comes from recognizing the diverse ways they process and apply knowledge. Howard Gardner's Multiple Intelligences Theory expands this understanding by identifying eight different forms of intelligence, each shaping how a student interacts with the world. When you integrate these intelligences into your teaching, you create a classroom where every student feels valued, engaged, and empowered to succeed.

Gardner's eight intelligences highlight the unique strengths of learners.

- ✓ Linguistic learners excel in reading, writing, and verbal expression, making them strong in storytelling and debate.

- ✓ Logical-mathematical learners thrive on critical thinking, numbers, and problem-solving, preferring structured challenges and logical reasoning.

- ✓ Spatial learners are visually oriented, excelling in design, maps, and artistic representation.

- ✓ Musical learners process information best through rhythm, melody, and sound, often using music as a memory aid.

✓ Bodily-kinaesthetic learners understand concepts through movement and physical interaction, engaging best in hands-on activities and role-playing.

✓ Interpersonal learners thrive in social settings, preferring group discussions, peer teaching, and collaborative projects.

✓ Intrapersonal learners, on the other hand, prefer independent study and self-reflection, absorbing knowledge best through journaling or introspective learning.

✓ Lastly, naturalistic learners connect with the world through nature and real-world applications, making them more responsive to outdoor learning experiences, environmental studies, and observation-based lessons.

To bring multiple intelligences to life in your classroom, consider integrating activities that cater to different strengths. Linguistic learners can write poems or speeches on lesson topics, while logical-mathematical learners can engage in problem-solving exercises. Spatial learners can create visual models or design presentations to demonstrate understanding, and musical learners can develop mnemonic songs to retain key concepts. Kinesthetic learners benefit from hands-on experiments and dramatizations, while interpersonal learners thrive in group projects and peer discussions. Intrapersonal learners can reflect through journaling or independent study, and naturalistic learners can deepen their understanding through nature-based projects.

By embracing multiple intelligences in your teaching, you go beyond traditional learning styles and unlock the full potential of your students. When you recognize and nurture these diverse strengths, you transform your classroom into a dynamic learning space where every student can shine. Teaching becomes more than just delivering lessons—it becomes an opportunity to ignite curiosity, foster creativity, and inspire lifelong learning.

Chapter 8
Unleashing The Power of Metacognition In The Classroom

When teachers unleash the power of metacognition, they don't just teach students what to learn—they empower them with the wisdom of how to think, reflect, and grow beyond the classroom.

Have you ever wondered why some students seem to grasp new concepts effortlessly while others struggle despite putting in the same amount of effort? What if I told you that the secret to learning success isn't just about intelligence or hard work but about knowing *how* to learn?

Metacognition may sound like a complex academic term, but at its core, it is a simple and powerful tool that can transform your teaching and, more importantly, your students' ability to learn independently. Imagine a classroom where students don't just memorize facts but actively *think* about *their thinking*—where they question their understanding, evaluate their learning strategies, and make adjustments to improve. When students develop metacognitive skills, they take charge of their own learning, making them more confident, capable, and self-sufficient learners.

In this chapter, you will explore what metacognition is, why it is crucial for student success, and how you can integrate it into your teaching in practical and meaningful ways.

The Hidden Key to Learning

Metacognition may sound like a complicated term, but in reality, it is one of the most powerful tools you can use as a teacher to transform the way your students learn. Think of it as a secret superpower—one that, when unlocked, helps your students take charge of their learning, think more deeply, and develop the confidence to tackle any challenge that comes their way.

At its core, metacognition is about thinking about thinking. It's the ability to step back, reflect, and ask, *How am I learning? What's working for me? What isn't? What can I do better?* When your students develop this skill, they don't just memorize facts; they become independent learners who can adapt, solve problems, and approach their studies with a sense of purpose.

Imagine how different your classroom would be if your students didn't just follow instructions blindly but instead became active participants in their own learning journey. What if they could recognize their strengths, identify their weaknesses, and adjust their approach when they encountered difficulties? That's what metacognition makes possible—and you have the power to guide them toward it.

The Power of Self-Awareness

One of the biggest challenges in education is that students often go through the motions of learning without really thinking about *how* they learn. They study for a test, take notes, and complete assignments, but they rarely stop to consider whether their methods are effective. This is where you come in.

You can teach your students to develop self-awareness about their learning process, and when that happens, everything changes. They start recognizing the difference between mindlessly reading a textbook and actively engaging with the material. They begin asking themselves important questions: *Am I understanding this concept, or am I just reading the words? What strategy should I use to remember this better? If I get stuck, how can I approach the problem differently?*

When your students start thinking in this way, they build a sense of control over their learning. No longer do they feel lost or helpless when faced with a difficult subject. Instead, they develop the ability to pause, reassess, and adjust their approach—just like a skilled navigator who changes course when faced with an unexpected roadblock. You have the ability to foster this mindset in your students, helping them move from uncertainty to confidence.

Breaking Free from Passive Learning

Too often, students rely on surface-level learning techniques. They highlight everything in their textbooks, reread the same paragraphs multiple times, or try to memorize long lists of information without truly understanding them. Then, when the test comes, they struggle to recall key ideas or apply their knowledge in a meaningful way.

Metacognition breaks this cycle, and you are the one who can help make that shift. You can teach your students to be active learners—to take charge of their education instead of waiting for knowledge to be handed to them. Instead of reading a chapter mindlessly, they can learn to stop and summarize it in their own words. Instead of cramming for an exam, they can practice recalling information and testing themselves. Instead of giving up when a concept feels difficult, they can reflect on why they are struggling and adjust their strategy.

This shift from passive to active learning is what separates students who simply get by from those who truly thrive. It's the difference between someone who follows a recipe without understanding why certain ingredients are used and someone who becomes a master chef, able to experiment and create their own dishes. You have the power to help your students develop this deeper level of understanding.

The Magic of Taking Control

When your students develop metacognitive skills, they move from being passive recipients of knowledge to becoming engaged, independent thinkers. They begin to understand that learning isn't about how much time they spend with their books open—it's about *how* they use that time.

A student who understands metacognition will approach studying differently. Instead of rereading the same material over and over, they might quiz themselves or teach the concept to a friend. Instead of feeling defeated by a low grade, they will analyze what went wrong and change their approach next time. They become problem-solvers, critical thinkers, and lifelong learners who can adapt to any situation.

And here's the best part: when your students start thinking about their thinking, they don't just perform better in school—they gain skills that will serve them for life. Whether they are learning a new subject, picking up a new skill, or navigating a challenge in their personal lives, the ability to reflect, adjust, and improve will always be invaluable.

Why Metacognition is a Game-Changer in Your Classroom

As a teacher, you don't just want your students to memorize facts—you want them to understand, apply, and retain what they've learned. You want them to think for themselves, make connections, and approach challenges with confidence. That's where metacognition comes in.

Think about two students preparing for a history exam. The first student reads the textbook repeatedly, highlighting nearly everything in bright yellow. They tell themselves, *The more I read, the more I'll remember.* The second student, however, takes a different approach. After reading each section, they pause and ask themselves: *What were the key points? How does this connect to what I already know? Can I explain this in my own words?*

Which student do you think will actually remember and understand the material better?

The answer is clear—the second student is engaging in metacognitive thinking. They actively monitor their learning, reflecting on what they know and adjusting their strategies based on their understanding. That is exactly the kind of learning you want to inspire in your classroom.

Students who develop metacognitive skills don't just do well on tests—they learn how to learn. They take control of their education, no longer just waiting for you to tell them what to do. They become curious thinkers, problem-solvers, and adaptable learners who thrive in and beyond the classroom.

Metacognition isn't just another educational buzzword—it's a transformational shift in the way students engage with learning. When you help your students develop metacognitive habits, you are giving them the tools to succeed in any subject, any challenge, and any situation. Here's why it matters so much in your classroom:

It Promotes Independent Learning – Imagine a classroom where students don't rely on you for every answer but instead take charge of their learning. Metacognition helps students develop self-awareness, so they can recognize what works best for them and refine their approach—without waiting for instructions.

It Increases Academic Achievement – Students who regulate their learning perform better on assignments and exams, but more importantly, they retain knowledge longer. Instead of cramming for a test and forgetting everything the next day, they build a deep understanding that lasts.

It Develops Critical Thinking Skills – You want your students to go beyond memorization, right? Metacognitive students ask deeper questions, analyze problems from multiple angles, and make informed decisions—skills that will serve them in every area of life.

It Builds Resilience – When students struggle, their first instinct is often frustration. But metacognitive students don't give up. Instead of saying, *I don't get this,* they think, *What strategy can I use to approach this differently?* They learn from their mistakes, adjust their strategies, and grow stronger.

When your students become metacognitive learners, they don't just survive in school—they flourish.

Now, take a moment and imagine your classroom filled with confident, engaged, and self-directed learners. Imagine students who no longer panic before a test but instead approach studying strategically and purposefully. Imagine learners who don't get discouraged by setbacks but instead use them as stepping stones toward growth. When you introduce your students to metacognitive strategies, you are changing the way they think, learn, and grow. You are giving them a gift that goes beyond the classroom—a mindset that will empower them for life.

So, as you step into your classroom tomorrow, ask yourself: How can I help my students think about their thinking today? Because once they do, their learning—and their future—will never be the same.

Chapter 9
Restoring The Brain For Learning Through Sleep

A well-rested brain is a learning brain—when teachers prioritize rest,
they teach students that growth happens not just in
study but also in sleep.

In today's fast-paced world, sleep is often treated as an afterthought, something to be sacrificed for productivity, lesson planning, and even late-night grading. It's not uncommon to hear students or teachers say, *"I only need five hours of sleep to function,"* as though sleep is a luxury rather than a necessity. But what if we've been looking at it all wrong? What if, instead of being a passive state of rest, sleep is actually the brain's most powerful and underappreciated tool for learning and teaching effectiveness?

As teachers, you are not just imparting knowledge—you are shaping minds. But how often do you and your students prioritize sleep as part of the learning process? Neuroscientific research reveals that sleep is not just about rest; it is the brain's powerhouse for memory consolidation, emotional balance, and cognitive performance. Without it, memory weakens, emotions become harder to manage, creativity is stifled, and overall learning suffers. The consequences of neglecting sleep affect both students and teachers alike, making it a critical issue in education.

The Overlooked Miracle of Memory Consolidation

It's a familiar scenario—students stay up late cramming for exams, believing that more hours awake equal more knowledge retained. Teachers, too, often sacrifice sleep to prepare lessons, evaluate assignments, or catch up on academic research. But what if this approach is doing more harm than good?

During sleep, the brain engages in memory consolidation—a process that stabilizes and stores new information for long-term use. This is when the brain sorts through the day's experiences, strengthens neural connections, and secures learning. Without sufficient sleep, this essential process is disrupted, leaving new knowledge fragile and easily forgotten. Imagine trying to save a file on a computer without clicking *"save"* or closing a document without backing it up—the data simply isn't secured.

As a teacher, you can encourage your students to study smarter, not longer, by prioritizing quality sleep. Research consistently shows that students who sleep after learning retain significantly more information than those who push through exhaustion. Deep sleep (slow-wave sleep) is responsible for storing facts and figures, while Rapid Eye Movement (REM) sleep enhances creative problem-solving. Without both, learning suffers.

The Emotional and Creative Power of REM Sleep

It's easy to dismiss sleep as downtime, but during REM sleep—the stage associated with vivid dreams—the brain is highly active. This phase plays a crucial role in processing emotions and fostering creativity. Have you ever woken up with a sudden solution to a problem or a fresh idea for a lesson? That's REM sleep at work.

For students under stress, REM sleep is particularly important. It helps regulate emotional responses, making it easier to process difficult experiences. Without it, frustration, anxiety, and even burnout become more common—major obstacles to academic success.

As a teacher, you can emphasize the importance of sleep in stress management. Students facing exams, presentations, or high-pressure coursework often feel they don't have time for rest. However, prioritizing sleep leads to better emotional regulation, sharper thinking, and enhanced problem-solving abilities. A well-rested student is not just more focused but also more innovative and resilient.

How Sleep Deprivation Derails Learning Across Ages

The impact of sleep deprivation is not limited to students; it affects teachers, parents, and lifelong learners alike. Whether it's a child staying up too late on a device, a teenager scrolling through social media at midnight, or an teacher sacrificing sleep for work, the consequences are profound.

For young children, lack of sleep interferes with brain development, language acquisition, and emotional regulation. Studies show that sleep-deprived children struggle with focus, learning new skills, and managing emotions.

For teenagers, academic pressure, digital distractions, and hormonal changes disrupt sleep cycles. Sleep deprivation during adolescence is linked to lower academic performance, increased stress, and higher rates of anxiety and depression.

For teachers, chronic sleep loss affects teaching effectiveness. Exhaustion reduces patience, impairs decision-making, and makes lesson planning feel overwhelming. Teachers who consistently lack sleep struggle with memory recall, creative lesson delivery, and emotional resilience in the classroom.

As a teacher, you set the tone for your students. By modeling healthy sleep habits and advocating for its importance, you help create a culture where rest is seen as an essential component of success, not a luxury.

Sleep Hygiene

Good sleep hygiene—the habits and practices that promote quality sleep—is essential for both students and teachers. Encouraging students to maintain a consistent sleep routine can significantly enhance their focus, memory, and overall well-being. Here's how you can guide your students toward better sleep:

Promote Consistent Sleep Schedules: Encourage students to go to bed and wake up at the same time every day. Irregular sleep patterns can disrupt the body's natural rhythm.

Limit Screen Time Before Bed: The blue light from phones and laptops interferes with melatonin production, making it harder to fall asleep. Encourage students to disconnect at least an hour before bedtime.

Create a Relaxing Bedtime Routine: Reading a book, practicing deep breathing, or journaling can help transition the brain into sleep mode.

Educate on Caffeine and Late-Night Snacking: Late-night stimulants, including caffeine and sugar, can interfere with deep sleep.

For teachers, prioritizing sleep can feel challenging with workload demands, but small changes can make a difference. Setting boundaries on work hours, practicing mindfulness before bed, and ensuring your sleep environment is comfortable can significantly improve rest quality.

A well-rested teacher is more patient, more engaging, and more effective in the classroom.

Reclaiming the Power of Sleep in an Overstimulated World

Sleep is often treated as a secondary priority, something to be sacrificed for extra study time, work, or entertainment. But this mindset comes at a cost—especially in education. From childhood to adulthood, sleep is the foundation for cognitive development, emotional balance, and creative problem-solving.

As a teacher, you have the power to shape not just what your students learn, but *how* they learn. By reinforcing the value of sleep, you help them develop lifelong habits that support academic success and personal well-being. Imagine a classroom where students come in well-rested, focused, and ready to absorb new information. Imagine a faculty where teachers are energized, patient, and innovative.

It all starts with a simple shift: valuing rest as much as effort. **Sleep is not lost time; it is a strategic investment in learning, teaching, and overall growth.** The journey to mastery, resilience, and well-being begins with prioritizing sleep.

Chapter 10

Understanding Gen Z, Gen Alpha, and Gen Beta

Teaching Gen Z, Gen Alpha, and Gen Beta means embracing change, adapting to new ways of thinking, and guiding them with wisdom that bridges the past, present, and future.

Welcome to a revolutionary era in education—a time when our learners are shaped by unprecedented advancements in technology, social shifts, and global interconnectedness. This chapter is a must-read if you're a teacher committed to making a difference. Understanding the unique traits and needs of Gen Z, Gen Alpha, and the emerging Gen Beta isn't just an option—it's essential for connecting with your students, engaging them meaningfully, and preparing them for the challenges ahead.

For years, teaching strategies have been tailored to the needs of past generations. However, the landscape of education is evolving faster than ever. Today's students are digital natives, immersed in technology every moment, and their learning preferences are shifting just as rapidly. It's time to move beyond traditional methods and adopt an approach that truly connects with the hearts and minds of the students before you. Let's attempt to understand the evolving traits of Gen Z, Gen Alpha, and the upcoming Gen Beta.

Know your learners Gen Z

Born between 1997 and 2012, Gen Z is the first true generation of digital natives. Unlike previous generations, they have never known a world without the internet, smartphones, or social media. Technology isn't just a tool for them—it's woven into every aspect of their lives. With information available at lightning speed, their expectations for learning are high. They crave quick, efficient, and interactive experiences that match the fast-paced digital landscape they navigate daily.

Gen Z is always connected, and that shapes how they learn. Traditional lecture-based teaching simply won't hold their attention. To truly engage them, teachers must incorporate multimedia tools like videos, podcasts, apps, and social learning platforms. These digital tools mirror the interactive world they are accustomed to, making learning feel more natural and immersive.

While often labelled as having short attention spans, Gen Z possesses an incredible ability to focus when something truly captivates them. The key is to spark their curiosity with content that is relevant, interactive, and thought-provoking. They thrive on real-world applications, critical thinking challenges, and problem-solving tasks that make them active participants in the learning process.

Despite their strong sense of independence, Gen Z is not a generation of lone learners. They excel in collaborative environments where they can exchange ideas, co-create content, and learn from their peers. They want the freedom to explore concepts on their own terms, but they also value community-driven learning experiences. As a teacher, your challenge is to strike the perfect balance—designing lessons that allow them to take ownership of their learning while fostering meaningful collaboration.

To teach Gen Z effectively, teachers must meet them where they are—deeply immersed in a digital world, eager to engage, and ready to learn through dynamic, interactive experiences. Traditional teaching methods alone won't capture their attention; instead, educators need to adapt their strategies, integrate technology seamlessly, and create lessons that are both relevant and engaging. By doing so, teachers can inspire curiosity, foster critical thinking, and help Gen Z thrive in the classroom.

To truly connect with Gen Z, you must **speak their language**—leveraging digital tools, incorporating real-world problem-solving, and designing lessons that encourage creativity and collaboration. When learning feels meaningful and applicable to their lives, Gen Z students become more motivated, engaged, and proactive. By embracing technology and student-centered approaches, you can transform their classrooms into innovative spaces where knowledge is not just absorbed but actively explored and applied.

Know your learners Gen Alpha

Born between 2013 and 2024, Gen Alpha is the first generation to be fully immersed in a digital world from birth. They've grown up in homes filled with smart devices, voice-activated assistants like Alexa and Siri, and on-demand access to information. By the time they step into the classroom, they will have already engaged with technology in ways that previous generations couldn't have imagined. Their expectations for education are not just high—they are revolutionary. They expect learning to be seamless, personalized, and as engaging as the digital experiences they encounter daily.

Gen Alpha thrives on learning through play. From the moment they can hold a device, they are engaging with interactive apps and educational games that make learning feel like an adventure. Gamification isn't just a trend for them—it's how they process and retain information. Traditional methods won't hold their attention; instead, they need immersive, experience-based learning that aligns with the digital-first world they navigate effortlessly.

Long lectures and static textbooks won't work with Gen Alpha. They are visual and interactive learners who absorb information best through dynamic, multi-sensory experiences. Their minds are wired for engagement through videos, augmented reality (AR), virtual reality (VR), and hands-on activities that make learning tangible and exciting. Instant feedback is crucial for them—they're used to real-time responses from their apps and games, and they expect the same level of interaction in the classroom.

Collaboration is second nature to Gen Alpha, but with a unique twist—they are global learners. Unlike previous generations, they aren't just social within their immediate surroundings; they are connecting with peers worldwide through digital platforms. Whether through gaming, social media, or virtual classrooms, they value cross-cultural interactions and expect learning environments to reflect this global perspective.

For Gen Alpha, the classroom should be a space for discovery, creativity, and problem-solving. Simply delivering information isn't enough; they need opportunities to explore, experiment, and co-create using the very tools that shape their everyday lives. By embracing interactive technology, fostering creativity, and designing learning experiences that feel as natural as their digital world, teachers can truly unlock the potential of this generation. Meet them where they are, and you won't just capture their attention—you'll prepare them for a rapidly evolving future where adaptability, innovation, and collaboration are key.

For Gen Alpha, your teaching must go beyond digital integration—it must be immersive, interactive, and exploratory. These young learners thrive on hands-on experiences, gamified learning, and real-time feedback. You should embrace augmented reality (AR), virtual reality (VR), and adaptive learning platforms that personalize their educational journey. Teaching Gen Alpha effectively means making learning feel like an adventure—one that fuels their natural curiosity and equips them with the skills they need for a rapidly changing future. By embracing these innovative approaches, you can create a learning environment where Gen Alpha students feel empowered, inspired, and ready to shape the world ahead.

Know your learners Gen Beta

Born between 2025 and 2039, Gen Beta will grow up in a world where artificial intelligence, robotics, and hyper-personalized learning are deeply embedded in daily life. Unlike previous generations, your students won't just use technology—they will interact with it in ways that reshape learning itself. Education for Gen Beta will be fluid, adaptive, and AI-driven, evolving with their individual needs. They won't simply absorb knowledge; they will co-create their learning experiences using AI-powered tools, immersive virtual environments, and real-time feedback mechanisms.

As a teacher, you play a crucial role in shaping this transformative learning journey. AI-personalized learning will become a powerful foundation for education, offering new possibilities to engage and support each student. Imagine a classroom where every learner has an AI tutor that adapts to their unique style, pace, and interests. With real-time analytics at your fingertips, you will be able to recognize strengths, address challenges, and design customized learning pathways. The traditional one-size-fits-all approach may gradually fade, making way for student-centered learning that nurtures autonomy, creativity, and critical thinking.

For Gen Beta, technology will be second nature. Virtual and augmented reality, AI-driven simulations, and gamified learning will seamlessly blend into their educational experiences. Your classroom will extend far beyond four walls, connecting students to global learning networks where they can collaborate with peers and experts worldwide. While previous generations viewed international collaboration as an opportunity, Gen Beta will see it as an essential part of their learning and future careers.

However, while technology will shape their world, human skills will define their success. Creativity, emotional intelligence, ethical reasoning, and adaptability will be more important than ever. Your role will evolve beyond that of a knowledge provider—you will become a mentor and guide, helping students balance digital fluency with deeper thinking and meaningful problem-solving.

To support Gen Beta effectively, embracing technology is just the beginning. Creating an environment where students feel encouraged to question, explore, innovate, and collaborate will be key. By thoughtfully integrating AI-driven tools while fostering human connection, ethical awareness, and adaptability, you will empower this generation with the skills they need to navigate and lead in a rapidly changing world. Your dedication and passion will make all the difference in shaping a future where learning is engaging, meaningful, and full of possibilities.

Why Understanding These Generations Matters for You as a Teacher

Understanding the unique traits of Gen Z, Gen Alpha, and Gen Beta isn't just about adjusting your teaching methods—it's about reimagining the entire learning experience. Each generation learns differently, and recognizing their needs will help you create a classroom environment that fosters engagement, creativity, and critical thinking.

Stay Ahead of the Curve: The world is changing rapidly. By understanding the key characteristics of your students, you position yourself as a forward-thinking teacher who can anticipate their needs, embrace technology, and adapt your teaching style to maximize learning outcomes.

Engage, Motivate, and Inspire: When you speak your students' language, use tools they are familiar with, and challenge them in ways that feel relevant, you ignite their curiosity and motivation. This connection fosters deeper engagement and more meaningful learning experiences.

Be the Teacher They Need: Each generation has its own strengths, struggles, and aspirations. Your role is to guide, inspire, and equip them with the skills they need to succeed—not just academically but as future leaders in a complex, interconnected world.

By understanding Gen Z, Gen Alpha, and Gen Beta, you aren't just preparing for today's classroom—you're preparing for the classrooms of the future. These generations aren't defined by technology alone—they are defined by their potential to change the world. As their teachers, you have the power to shape that future. Embrace the challenge, adapt your teaching, and become the catalyst for their success. Together, we can build learning experiences that resonate with these digital natives and prepare them to thrive in an ever-evolving world.

* * *

Section III
Teaching Mastery

(Developing core teaching strategies for modern classrooms)

Teaching Mastery

Teaching mastery is not about knowing it all but about continually learning, adapting, and inspiring students to think, question, and grow.

Teaching is not just a job—it's a profound art, science, and calling. It is the bridge between knowledge and transformation, between inspiration and action. Have you ever wondered what truly makes a great teacher? Is it knowledge? Skill? Or something deeper—perhaps the ability to ignite minds, shape futures, and awaken the limitless potential in others?

At the core of teaching mastery lies the Guru-Sishya bond, a timeless connection that goes beyond textbooks and lectures. A teacher doesn't just impart knowledge; they cultivate curiosity, nurture resilience, and instil a love for learning. But as education continues to evolve—shaped by technology, shifting student needs, and new methodologies—so must the teacher. Are you ready to evolve with it?

Mastering the art of teaching is about adaptability and lifelong learning. In a world where AI is reshaping education, where students learn in new and dynamic ways, and where attention spans are constantly challenged, the best teachers are those who embrace change while staying rooted in timeless educational values. Whether it's integrating digital tools, fostering deep thinking, or creating meaningful connections in hybrid classrooms, teaching mastery requires both skill and heart.

This section is designed to inspire, challenge, and empower you. Through practical strategies, real-world insights, and powerful reflections, you will strengthen your ability to motivate, engage, and transform. More importantly, you'll realize that your presence, your passion, and your belief in your students hold the power to shape their lives.

Chapter 11
Shaping The Thinkers of Tomorrow

Teachers don't just share knowledge—they shape the thinkers of tomorrow by igniting curiosity, fostering resilience, and inspiring a lifelong love for learning.

The essence of education is not just to fill minds with information but to ignite the flames of curiosity, critical thinking, and lifelong learning. In a world driven by rapid technological advancements and an overwhelming flow of information, your students need more than just knowledge—they need the ability to think, analyze, question, and innovate.

As a teacher, you are not merely delivering lessons; you are shaping the next generation of thinkers, problem-solvers, and leaders. Regardless of the resources available in your classroom, what truly makes a difference is the mindset you cultivate. The way you encourage curiosity, facilitate discussions, and challenge students to think beyond the obvious defines their learning journey.

So, how can you ensure that your students develop the skills they need to navigate the complexities of the modern world? It starts with simple but powerful shifts in the way you teach.

Encourage Inquiry

The best lessons start not with answers, but with great questions. The ability to ask meaningful questions is the foundation of critical thinking and independent learning. If your students only memorize information without questioning it, they miss the opportunity to truly understand and apply knowledge.

To foster inquiry-based learning, you must shift from simply delivering facts to encouraging curiosity. When you create a space where students feel safe to ask questions, explore ideas, and challenge assumptions, you empower them to take ownership of their learning.

Instead of: *"Here is what you need to know."* Try: *"What do you think? How can we find out? What are the possible perspectives?"* By shifting from giving information to stimulating curiosity, you help students develop a habit of thinking deeply and critically.

Use the **Socratic Method**—ask open-ended, thought-provoking questions that require students to analyze and justify their responses. Example: Instead of asking, *"What are the causes of climate change?"* try, *"If you were a world leader, how would you address climate change?"* When you encourage students to challenge assumptions, debate ideas, and explore different viewpoints, you cultivate independent thinkers who are not afraid to question the world around them.

Connect Learning to Real-World Issues

Learning becomes more meaningful when students see its relevance to their lives and the world around them. As a teacher, you have the power to bridge classroom concepts with real-world applications, making lessons come alive.

✓ **Why it works:** When students see that what they are learning applies to real life, they engage more deeply and develop a stronger sense of purpose.

✓ **How to do it:** Use case studies, current events, and hands-on projects to apply concepts to real-life problems.

Instead of just teaching mathematical probability, have students analyze real-world statistics—such as predicting election outcomes or studying trends in climate data. When you show students the real-world impact of their learning, you inspire them to think critically and take ownership of their knowledge.

Foster a Culture of Debate and Discussion

A classroom that values discussion over passive learning is a classroom that fosters deep thinking. Encouraging debate and discussion allows students to refine their ideas, listen critically, and articulate their thoughts effectively. Encourage students to challenge ideas, engage in debates, and articulate their perspectives. When students learn to support their viewpoints with logic and evidence, they become more confident and independent thinkers.

✓ Use structured debates to help students develop logical arguments, back up claims with evidence, and respectfully critique opposing viewpoints.

✓ After reading a novel or studying a historical event, assign students different perspectives and have them defend their stance in a formal debate.

When you create an environment where students feel comfortable expressing their opinions and analyzing different viewpoints, you nurture open-minded, critical thinkers.

Emphasize Problem-Solving and Creativity

Innovation thrives when students are encouraged to think outside the box. Problem-solving activities challenge students to apply their knowledge creatively and independently. Instead of giving them all the answers, allow them to struggle, experiment, and discover solutions on their own.

Instead of: *"Here's how to do it."* Try: *"Here's the problem—how would you solve it?"*

Encourage project-based learning, where students research, design, and present their own solutions to complex problems. Example: In a science class, instead of explaining renewable energy, ask students to design their own sustainable energy solutions for their community.

When students actively engage in problem-solving, they internalize learning in a way that no lecture ever could. By fostering creativity in your classroom, you prepare students to tackle the unpredictable challenges of the future.

Teach Students to Analyze Media and Information Critically

In a world overflowing with information, students must learn to evaluate sources, detect bias, and differentiate fact from misinformation. This skill is crucial in an era where social media, fake news, and AI-generated content can blur the lines between truth and manipulation.

- ✓ **Strategy:** Implement media literacy activities where students analyze news articles, advertisements, and social media posts for credibility, bias, and intent.

- ✓ **Example:** Ask students to compare multiple news sources on the same event and discuss the differences in framing, language, and evidence.

By equipping your students with critical media analysis skills, you empower them to become informed, responsible citizens who can navigate the digital age with confidence.

Model Curiosity and a Growth Mindset

As a teacher, you are not just imparting knowledge—you are modelling lifelong learning. When you demonstrate curiosity, adaptability, and a willingness to learn, your students will follow your lead.

- ✓ Admit when you don't know something.

- ✓ Share your excitement for discovery.

- ✓ Encourage persistence and resilience in the face of challenges.

When students see that learning is a lifelong journey, they will embrace challenges rather than fear them. Your mindset shapes theirs.

As a teacher, your influence extends far beyond textbooks and exams. You are shaping minds, perspectives, and futures. Every question you ask, every challenge you present, every discussion you spark—it all contributes to moulding the leaders of tomorrow.

- ✓ When you teach a student to question deeply, you give them the power to navigate an uncertain world.

- ✓ When you challenge them to think critically, you equip them to solve real-world problems.

- ✓ When you awaken their curiosity, you ignite a lifelong love for learning.

The future belongs to those who can think beyond boundaries, solve problems, and innovate. And that journey starts with you.

Chapter 12
You Are The Most Important Tech In The Classroom

In a world of ever-evolving technology, the most powerful tool in the classroom is still the teacher—innovative, adaptable, and deeply human.

Do you know? The digital revolution isn't some distant future—it's happening now, reshaping the way we teach and learn. But here's the truth: no app, AI tool, or gadget can ever replace the impact of a passionate, engaged teacher. Technology is just a tool—it's YOU who makes the difference.

So, step into this digital world with confidence. Experiment, explore, and use technology not just to teach but to inspire. Your students are already immersed in a tech-driven world; with the right mindset, you can meet them there and guide them to use it meaningfully.

You've spent years honing your craft—connecting with students, sparking curiosity, and making learning come alive. Technology doesn't change that. It enhances what you already do best. Digital tools aren't here to replace your wisdom, your intuition, or the special bond you build with your students. They're here to support you—to help you bring lessons to life in new and exciting ways.

Think about the possibilities. With gamification, you can turn learning into an adventure. With adaptive technology, you can reach every student at their own pace. With multimedia storytelling, you can make even the most complex topics engaging and relatable. But here's the key: you are the one shaping how students interact with technology. It's your guidance, not the tool itself, that makes learning meaningful.

And just as you encourage your students to keep learning, you, too, must grow. Digital literacy, online safety, and responsible content creation aren't just skills—they're necessities in today's classrooms. The tools will keep evolving, but your ability to adapt, innovate, and inspire will always be the most powerful force in your classroom.

Remember this: The most important technology in your classroom isn't a device or an app—it's YOU. Your creativity, your presence, and your passion for teaching are what truly make the difference. So, let's explore how you can bring technology into your teaching with confidence and creativity:

Flip Your Classroom for Active Learning: Why spend valuable class time explaining concepts that your students can explore independently? Instead, let them engage with instructional content before class through videos, podcasts, or online readings. Platforms like Khan Academy, DIKSHA, and YouTube Education provide high-quality lessons that your students can access at their own pace. This flipped approach frees up your class time for deeper discussions, group work, and hands-on problem-solving—where real learning happens. You can use Google Classroom or Microsoft Teams to organize content and track student progress effectively.

Gamify Teaching for More Engagement: Games make learning interactive and enjoyable. Instead of traditional quizzes, turn assessments into exciting challenges using Kahoot! and Quizizz, which help test your students' knowledge in a fun and competitive way. You can also design digital scavenger hunts or classroom challenges using

Google Forms. Rewarding your students with leaderboards, badges, or interactive elements makes learning feel like an adventure, keeping them motivated while reinforcing key concepts.

Encourage Collaboration Beyond Your Classroom: Collaboration should not be limited to your classroom walls. Encourage your students to work together in real-time using Google Docs, OneNote, and Padlet for brainstorming and group projects. Assign creative tasks such as digital posters, infographics, and presentations using Canva to help your students develop digital storytelling skills. Encouraging them to co-write reports, essays, or research papers nurtures teamwork and communication—essential skills that will serve them beyond academics.

Make Your Assessments Smarter and More Interactive: Assessments should go beyond rote memorization and provide meaningful insights. Use Mentimeter or Google Forms to conduct live class polls and gather instant feedback. AI-driven tools such as Turnitin help maintain academic integrity, while Google Classroom's quiz feature enables you to create adaptive quizzes tailored to your students' needs. Personalized assessments allow your students to learn from their mistakes in real time, making evaluations more constructive and student-friendly.

Bring Your Lessons to Life with AR and VR: Why just teach about history, science, or geography when your students can experience it? Augmented and virtual reality make abstract concepts more tangible and engaging. Google Arts and Culture offers virtual field trips to historical sites, while Merge Cube and Quiver allow your students to interact with 3D models of scientific concepts. For STEM subjects (Science, Technology, Engineering, and Mathamatics), PhET Simulations provide hands-on digital experiments that improve understanding of complex topics.

Use AI and Adaptive Learning for Personalized Education: Every student learns at a different pace, and AI-powered tools can help personalize their learning experience. Language learners can benefit from Duolingo, and platforms like Google Read Along enhance reading skills for younger students. Personalized AI-driven tutoring ensures that none of your students are left behind while allowing high achievers to advance at their own speed.

Encourage Your Students to Create Digital Content: Instead of being passive consumers, your students should be creators of knowledge. Encourage them to express their understanding through blog posts, podcasts, or short videos. Flipgrid enables interactive video discussions, while Canva allows them to design digital posters and infographics. Multimedia storytelling tools like Powtoon make presentations more engaging. By fostering digital creativity, you help your students develop essential 21st-century skills such as communication, critical thinking, and problem-solving.

Take Your Classroom Beyond the Walls: Technology provides opportunities to connect your students with the world. You can invite guest speakers or experts using Google Meet or Zoom, exposing your students to diverse perspectives. International collaborations through PenPal Schools or global competitions enhance learning beyond textbooks. Engaging your students in digital projects with peers from other schools fosters cultural exchange and broadens their understanding of global issues.

Blend Traditional and Digital Teaching Methods: Technology should not replace the great teaching methods you already use—it should enhance them. Combining face-to-face discussions with digital collaboration ensures a well-rounded learning experience. Interactive whiteboards, virtual simulations, and multimedia storytelling help engage your students in new ways while balancing screen time with hands-on activities. Thoughtfully integrating digital tools creates a dynamic and engaging classroom environment where both technology and traditional pedagogy work together for your students' success.

By incorporating these technology-driven strategies, you can transform your classroom into a space where engagement, creativity, and collaboration thrive. Whether you're flipping your lessons, gamifying learning, or using AI for personalized instruction, the goal remains the same: to make learning more meaningful and accessible for your students. Embrace technology as your ally, and watch your teaching—and your students—flourish!

Technology doesn't define great teaching—you do. The way you integrate, adapt, and innovate with digital tools will shape how your students learn, engage, and thrive in a connected world. So, learn alongside your students. Keep your curiosity, creativity, and passion at the heart of your teaching. The future belongs to teachers who are willing to lead, adapt, and inspire. And with the right mindset, you won't just keep up with the digital revolution—you'll be at the forefront of it.

Chapter 13
AI Is Your Ally, Not Your Replacement

AI can enhance teaching, but it can never replace the heart, wisdom, and inspiration of a great teacher because education is powered by human connection.

Artificial Intelligence is no longer a futuristic concept—it is here, transforming education in ways you never imagined. But rather than viewing AI as a threat, you must see it as an ally, a powerful tool that enhances rather than replaces the human touch in teaching. AI can assist with various aspects of education, but it cannot replicate the compassion, critical thinking, and inspiration that define great teaching.

The fear that AI will replace teachers is misplaced. AI cannot inspire curiosity, cultivate resilience, or ignite a student's passion for learning—only you can. Instead of seeing AI as a competitor, embrace it as a powerful assistant that lightens your administrative load, allowing you to focus more on meaningful interactions with students. AI can automate grading, provide instant feedback, and offer adaptive learning paths, but it is you who makes learning truly engaging and transformative.

By leveraging AI, you ensure that technology works for you—not the other way around. When used wisely, AI allows you to reclaim your time, making space for the moments that matter most—the conversations, the mentorship, and the creative learning experiences that shape students' lives.

Personalizing Learning with AI

Every student learns at a different pace, with unique strengths and challenges. AI has the potential to transform education by adapting lessons to individual needs, ensuring that no student is left behind. AI-driven platforms analyze student responses in real time, offering additional support or challenges where needed. This personalized approach helps bridge learning gaps and enhances student engagement.

However, AI is only a tool—it does not replace your ability to understand a student's emotions, struggles, and aspirations. AI can identify patterns, but it cannot sense when a student is feeling discouraged or unmotivated. That's where you come in. By integrating AI-driven learning assistants into your teaching strategies, you create a dynamic learning environment where students receive both personalized support from technology and the invaluable guidance that only you can provide.

Encourage students to use AI-powered learning assistants for practice and reinforcement, but always ensure that human interaction remains central to the learning experience. AI can provide data, but you provide wisdom. AI can highlight gaps in knowledge, but you help students overcome them with patience, encouragement, and real-world insights.

Teaching Digital Literacy and AI Ethics

In a world where AI-generated content is everywhere, your role as a teacher is more important than ever. You are not just teaching facts—

you are teaching students how to think critically, question information, and navigate a digital world filled with both possibilities and pitfalls. AI is only as good as the way it is used, and its outputs can sometimes be biased, inaccurate, or misleading.

Your students need to develop digital literacy skills to critically evaluate AI-generated content rather than accepting it at face value. One of the best ways to do this is by integrating discussions on AI ethics, algorithmic bias, and responsible digital citizenship into your lessons. Make this practical by having your students analyze AI-generated text for bias or misinformation and compare it with trusted sources. Encourage debates on ethical AI use, exploring both its benefits and risks.

By guiding your students to think critically and use AI wisely, you ensure that AI becomes a tool for learning rather than a crutch for easy answers. You empower them to ask the right questions, challenge assumptions, and develop a healthy scepticism toward technology—skills that are essential in today's information-rich world.

Encouraging Creativity in the Age of AI

Despite its many advantages, AI lacks originality, emotion, and true creativity—qualities that define human intelligence. AI can generate ideas, summarize content, and even create art, but it cannot replicate the depth of human imagination. That is why your role is to encourage students to go beyond AI-generated solutions and think independently. AI should serve as a tool for inspiration rather than a replacement for human creativity.

Challenge your students to refine AI-generated ideas, critique them, or use them as a starting point for their original work. For example, instead of having AI write an essay, ask your students to analyze AI-generated drafts and enhance them with their personal insights, arguments, and style. Have them push beyond AI-generated artwork by adding emotional depth and meaning. Encourage storytelling, experimentation, and self-expression in ways AI simply cannot replicate.

By fostering creativity, you ensure that students remain thinkers, innovators, and problem-solvers rather than passive consumers of technology. The future belongs to those who can use AI as a tool without losing their human spark—their ability to dream, imagine, and create something truly original.

Building Human Connections in a Tech-Driven Classroom

Education is not just about information—it is about relationships, mentorship, and inspiration. While AI can personalize learning experiences, it cannot replace the emotional connections that shape a student's character and motivation. Your greatest strength as a teacher lies in your ability to inspire, empathize, and guide students through their challenges.

To maintain this human connection, balance AI-assisted learning with interactive discussions, storytelling, and collaborative projects that build emotional intelligence and interpersonal skills. Encourage meaningful conversations, engage students in group activities, and use real-life examples to bring lessons to life. AI might provide personalized feedback, but it is your encouragement and belief in your students that truly motivates them to grow.

When students feel supported and understood, they develop confidence and a deeper love for learning—something no AI tool can provide. You are the heart of the classroom, the mentor who makes learning meaningful and memorable. AI can assist, but it is your connection with students that leaves a lasting impact.

The Architect of an AI-Empowered Future

You are not just teaching in the age of AI—you are shaping how students engage with it, ensuring they become responsible and ethical users of technology. With the right mindset, AI can become a powerful tool that amplifies your impact, making education more dynamic, inclusive, and effective.

The future of education is not about choosing between AI and teachers—it is about integrating both to create a richer, more engaging learning experience. You hold the key to this transformation by guiding students to think critically, use AI responsibly, and harness technology for meaningful learning.

- ✓ Embrace AI as an ally, not a rival.

- ✓ Use AI to enhance learning, not replace human connection.

- ✓ Empower students to be critical thinkers, ethical users, and creative problem-solvers.

- ✓ AI advancements to integrate them effectively.

By embracing AI as your ally, you empower yourself and your students to shape the future of education with confidence and creativity. The heart of learning will always be HUMAN, and YOU, as a teacher, will always be IRREPLACEABLE.

Chapter 14

Are You Truly Humanizing Your Online Classroom?

Technology connects us, but it's the teacher's warmth, empathy, and presence that truly humanize the online classroom.

Online teaching is no longer a novelty—it's an expectation. You have likely adapted to digital tools, mastered virtual platforms, and structured your courses for remote learning. But here's the real question: Are you truly humanizing online instruction, or have you simply transferred traditional methods into a digital space?

In a world where screens dominate communication and AI-generated responses are everywhere, your students don't just need well-organized lectures and neatly packaged content. They need connection. They need to know that behind the screen is a teacher who sees them, values them, and believes in their potential.

Students today are navigating more than just academic challenges. They are dealing with isolation, digital fatigue, and an overwhelming flood of information. The ease of online learning can sometimes make education feel transactional—log in, complete the work, log out. But where is the human connection in that? Your challenge is not just to instruct but to create an environment where students feel deeply engaged, supported, and inspired—despite the physical distance.

Think about it: What if the true test of online teaching is not how well you deliver content but how well you foster human formation and transformation in a virtual world? What if your greatest success is measured not in grades but in how connected, motivated, and empowered your students feel?

This chapter is not about what you already know. It's about pushing beyond the basics. It's about rethinking your role in the digital classroom—not as a content provider but as a teacher who breathes life into learning, builds relationships beyond the screen, and ensures that technology enhances—not replaces—the human touch.

So, ask yourself: Are you making your online classroom a place of true learning and connection? Or has it become just another screen in your students' daily routine? It's time to challenge yourself—to go beyond convenience and efficiency and create an online learning experience that is deeply human, profoundly engaging, and truly transformative.

Teaching with Presence

One of the greatest challenges of online instruction is the emotional gap between teachers and students. Without the warmth of face-to-face interaction, many students feel disconnected, unseen, and unmotivated. However, distance should never mean detachment. Just because you are physically apart does not mean you cannot create a deep, meaningful connection with your students. Your presence in an online classroom is not about proximity—it's about engagement, responsiveness, and your ability to make each student feel recognized, valued, and supported.

Students are more engaged and perform better in online courses when teachers demonstrate an active presence, show genuine care, and invest personally in their success. But what does presence really mean in an online setting? It's more than just logging in, posting announcements, or grading assignments. It's about showing up in ways that make students feel heard, understood, and encouraged to participate. Imagine how different a student's experience would be if, instead of just receiving automated feedback, they got a personalized message acknowledging their progress. What if, instead of feeling like they are studying in isolation, they felt part of a thriving, interactive learning community?

To bridge the digital divide and create a more human-centered online classroom, educators must move beyond transactional teaching and cultivate an atmosphere of trust, belonging, and engagement. One powerful strategy is personalized check-ins, where teachers dedicate time for one-on-one meetings or small group discussions to understand students' challenges, learning needs, and aspirations. Live Q&A sessions and open office hours also provide opportunities for students to share concerns, connect informally, and feel supported. Additionally, fostering a community-driven learning environment through discussion forums, peer collaborations, and student-led presentations helps transform learning into a shared experience. Celebrating student voices by showcasing their work, highlighting achievements, and acknowledging their efforts reinforces their confidence and motivation. In the end, while technology provides the platform, it is the teacher's presence that truly transforms the learning experience.

Overcoming Digital Fatigue

Let's be honest—staring at a screen for hours is mentally exhausting. Passive lectures, endless slideshows, and back-to-back virtual sessions can leave students feeling disconnected and drained, no matter how important the content is. Digital fatigue is real, and if it isn't addressed, students may lose focus before the lesson even begins. The constant demand to concentrate, process information, and engage in virtual discussions can be overwhelming. As a teacher, your challenge is to transform online learning into an active, engaging, and refreshing experience rather than a tiring one.

So, how can you counteract digital fatigue? Start by rethinking lesson structures. Shorter, high-impact sessions are more effective than lengthy lectures. Breaking content into bite-sized, interactive segments helps maintain attention and enhances retention. Incorporating multisensory learning—videos, animations, infographics, and storytelling—makes lessons more dynamic. Movement and mindfulness breaks are also crucial. Encouraging students to stretch, take a reflection break, or engage in a quick breathing exercise can reset their focus and prevent burnout.

Finally, give students creative freedom in demonstrating their learning. Instead of traditional assignments, let them create podcasts, vlogs, digital storytelling projects, or AI-assisted presentations. When students take ownership of their learning, their motivation increases. Now, reflect: What's one small change you can make to bring more energy and excitement into your next online session?

Shifting from Consumers to Co-Creators

In the most engaging online classrooms, students are not just passive recipients of information—they are active co-creators in the learning process. When they have a say in shaping their education, their motivation, confidence, and sense of ownership over their learning increase significantly. Traditional teacher-centered models, where the instructor controls the flow of knowledge, often leave students disengaged and dependent. However, shifting your role from a sole provider of knowledge to a guide for exploration empowers students to take charge of their learning. This transformation fosters deeper understanding, critical thinking, and a genuine connection to the subject matter. The goal is to move beyond content delivery and create opportunities for students to contribute meaningfully to their learning experience.

One of the most effective ways to encourage student-driven learning is by giving them space to lead. Allow them to choose discussion topics, design projects, or even teach mini-lessons to their peers. This approach enhances engagement while developing communication, collaboration, and leadership skills. Collaborative learning—through peer mentoring, co-authored digital materials, or team-based projects—further reinforces their role as active participants. Applying knowledge to real-world situations also makes learning more relevant and lasting. For instance, instead of writing a traditional research paper, students could create a podcast episode exploring practical applications of the concepts they've studied.

Now, reflect on your teaching approach. Are you primarily delivering information, or are you guiding exploration? Consider independently. When students shift from consumers of knowledge to co-creators, learning becomes more dynamic, meaningful, and transformative.

Beyond the Screen

At the heart of education lies transformation, not mere information. While students may eventually forget the specifics of a lesson, they will never forget the way you made them feel. The true impact of teaching is measured not by the number of slides presented or the amount of content covered but by the human connections you foster and the confidence you instil in your students. As an online teacher, your challenge is to bridge the emotional gap, ensuring that digital learning does not become a sterile, impersonal experience. Instead, it should be a space where students feel seen, heard, and valued—a space where learning is not just about acquiring knowledge but about growing as individuals.

Think about the students who enter your virtual classroom. Some may be struggling with self-doubt, questioning their abilities in an online world where interaction feels distant and impersonal. Others may feel invisible, lost in the sea of muted microphones and black screens. But then, something changes. A word of encouragement, a personal check-in, an acknowledgment of their ideas—small acts that rekindle confidence and motivation. Maybe it's the student who never spoke up before but finds their voice because you created a welcoming space. Maybe it's the learner who discovers a love for the subject because you brought energy, warmth, and authenticity into your teaching. These are not just moments—they are life-changing experiences that define the legacy of a truly impactful teacher.

The best teachers are not remembered for their lectures but for the way they made learning feel personal, powerful, and possible. As you move forward in your journey of online teaching, embrace innovation, deepen connections, and continue to inspire. Teaching beyond the screen is about more than adapting to technology—it's about humanizing education in a digital world. Your role is more important than ever, and your ability to bring warmth, empathy, and engagement into your virtual classroom can change lives.

- ✓ Keep innovating- Experiment with new ways to engage students and make learning immersive.

- ✓ Keep connecting - Prioritize relationships, empathy, and meaningful interactions.

- ✓ Keep inspiring - Your passion for teaching has the power to ignite curiosity and shape futures.

Teaching online is like lighting a candle in the dark—you may not see the glow immediately, but it can illuminate a student's path in ways you never imagined.

Chapter 15
You Are Unstoppable

Resilient teachers are the backbone of education. Not because they never struggle—but because they refuse to give up.

Change is the only constant in education. New technologies emerge, teaching methodologies evolve, and students bring with them fresh challenges and possibilities every year. A lesson plan that worked beautifully last semester might fall flat today. A well-structured schedule might be turned upside down overnight.

And yet, through all the shifts, one truth remains: a resilient teacher doesn't just endure change—they embrace it, adapt to it, and transform it into an opportunity for growth.

You didn't choose this profession because it was easy. You chose it because you believe in something bigger than yourself—the power of education to shape lives, ignite potential, and open doors to the future.

Resilience is not about pretending that challenges don't exist. It's about standing in the middle of them and saying, *"I will find a way forward."* It's about adjusting without losing your passion, shifting gears without losing sight of your purpose.

Think back to a moment when a lesson didn't go as planned, when technology failed in the middle of an important presentation, or when a student's struggle weighed heavily on your heart. And yet, you kept going. You adjusted. You found another way. That's resilience in action.

So how do we strengthen this quality and use it to not only survive but flourish?

Adaptability

Teaching is an ever-evolving journey. No two days in a classroom are the same, and the ability to adapt is what separates a good teacher from a great one. Whether it's a sudden schedule change, an unexpected student response, or a technology failure, your ability to pivot with confidence determines the effectiveness of your teaching. Adaptability isn't just about reacting to change—it's about embracing it as an opportunity for growth. When you model flexibility and problem-solving, your students learn to navigate challenges with resilience and confidence.

Instead of seeing disruptions as roadblocks, view them as detours to something new and valuable. If a lesson isn't landing, tweak it. If students seem disengaged, switch up your approach. The best teachers are problem-solvers, not perfectionists. No one has all the answers—not even the most experienced educator. Permit yourself to learn alongside your students. When you model curiosity and adaptability, they learn that growth is a lifelong process.

Not every day will go according to plan. Technology might fail, activities might take unexpected turns, and school policies might change. Being prepared for the unexpected makes all the difference. Keep backup strategies for lessons, assessments, and even your own mental well-being.

Teaching in the Face of Uncertainty

Education has undergone profound changes in recent years. The shift to digital learning, the integration of AI in classrooms, and the evolving needs of students require teachers to constantly adapt. It can feel overwhelming, but remember—you don't have to navigate these changes alone. The key to thriving in uncertain times lies in collaboration, purpose, and a willingness to innovate. Your ability to stay focused on your mission as an educator will help you overcome obstacles and find creative solutions.

You don't have to figure it all out yourself. Lean into collaboration. Find strength in your fellow educators. Share strategies, ask for advice, and support one another. A resilient teacher knows when to reach out.

Try and experiment boldly. Some of the greatest educational breakthroughs come from trying new things. Whether it's integrating a new teaching tool, flipping your classroom, or using storytelling in your lessons, step outside your comfort zone. Some ideas will work brilliantly; others may not. But every step is a step forward.

Nurturing Your Well-Being

As a teacher, you pour so much of yourself into your students, but resilience isn't just about pushing through difficult times—it's also about ensuring you have the strength to sustain yourself in the long run. A well-rested, motivated teacher is far more effective than one running on empty. Prioritizing your well-being isn't selfish; it's necessary for you to continue inspiring and leading your students. By setting boundaries, pursuing personal growth, and embracing small moments of joy, you can maintain your passion for teaching while avoiding burnout.

- ✓ **Please set boundaries** - Your time and energy are precious. It's okay to say no. Protect your evenings, weekends, and mental space so that you can show up as your best self.

- ✓ **Keep learning**- Resilient teachers never stop growing. Read books, listen to podcasts, take online courses—fuel your passion with new ideas.

✓ **Try to find joy in small moments-** A student's *"aha"* moment, a thoughtful thank-you note, a breakthrough with a struggling learner—these moments matter more than any curriculum or standardized test. Hold onto them. They are why you teach.

Turning Challenges into Opportunities

Every challenge in the classroom carries the seed of an opportunity. The best teachers don't see obstacles as limitations—they see them as chances to grow. Whether you're facing disengaged students, a lesson that isn't going as planned, or constantly evolving educational policies, your response makes all the difference. Instead of feeling defeated, shift your perspective and ask, *"How can I turn this into something positive?"* With the right mindset, even the toughest days become stepping stones toward better teaching.

✓ When the Students are disengaged - Experiment with interactive teaching methods, games, storytelling, or technology to reignite curiosity.

✓ When a lesson doesn't go as planned- Adapt in real-time, ask students for input, shift the discussion, or introduce a hands-on activity.

✓ When Educational policies and technology keep changing- Stay ahead by embracing professional development. The more you grow, the more confident you become.

Your Resilience Inspires Others

Every time you show resilience, you teach your students a lesson far beyond the curriculum. They watch how you handle stress, change, and failure, and in doing so, they learn the value of perseverance. Your ability to embrace challenges, keep learning, and find joy even in difficult times leaves a lasting impression. The lessons you teach through your own example will follow them long after they leave your classroom.

- ✓ When you show up with determination, they learn perseverance.
- ✓ When you embrace change with confidence, they learn adaptability.
- ✓ When you continue learning, they see that growth never stops.

Every time you push through difficulty, try something new, or find joy in the midst of uncertainty, you are teaching them a lesson that will last a lifetime.

And that, Dear Teacher, is the greatest gift you can give them.

Change is inevitable, and Growth is a choice

Change is an unavoidable part of life, but how you respond to it is always within your control. As a teacher, whether in a tech-enabled urban school or a resource-limited rural classroom, you constantly face new challenges that test your adaptability. The true mark of a teacher is not the tools they have but the mindset they bring to teaching.

Mr. Raj, a dedicated teacher in a government school, had been using traditional methods for years. Then, one day, his school introduced a new activity-based curriculum, requiring digital resources that weren't easily accessible in his classroom. Meanwhile, in a city school, Ms. Asha found herself struggling as well—her institution had shifted to AI-powered learning, and she felt overwhelmed by the sudden need to integrate technology into her teaching.

Both teachers faced a choice: resist change or embrace it.

Mr. Raj decided to innovate within his means. When digital tools weren't available, he used storytelling, peer teaching, and locally available materials to bring lessons to life. He collaborated with fellow teachers, borrowed ideas from training workshops, and transformed his classroom into an interactive learning space—without needing expensive gadgets.

Ms. Asha, on the other hand, leaned into learning new technology. She sought help from younger colleagues, attended online courses, and experimented with AI tools to personalize student learning. What once seemed intimidating soon became a powerful way to enhance engagement.

Months later, both teachers weren't just keeping up—they were thriving. Their students were more engaged, their lessons more dynamic, and they had rediscovered the joy of teaching.

Their stories remind us that resilience is not about resources but about resourcefulness. Whether you have the latest technology or just a chalkboard, the key to being unstoppable lies in your ability to adapt, innovate, and keep learning.

So, the next time change knocks on your classroom door, welcome it with open arms. Trust in your ability to grow, seek support when needed, and remember: you are not just teaching students—you are shaping the future.

No matter where you teach, you are unstoppable.

* * *

Section IV
Mastery Beyond the Blackboard

(Practical strategies for Tackling real-world classroom challenges with effective solutions)

Mastery Beyond The Blackboard

True teaching mastery goes beyond the blackboard—it lies in the ability to inspire, adapt, and shape lives both inside and outside the classroom.

Education is no longer confined to the blackboard or the pages of a textbook—it is about fostering curiosity, creativity, and critical thinking in students. In a world where knowledge is just a click away, where social media, artificial intelligence, and personalized digital tools are reshaping how students absorb information, traditional teaching methods often struggle to hold their attention.

As a teacher, you are no longer just a dispenser of facts—you are a leader, a supporter, and a trendsetter. Your challenge is not simply to deliver content but to create an experience that makes learning irresistible. How do you navigate the ever-growing distractions? How do you keep students engaged in an era of shrinking attention spans? How do you balance discipline with flexibility, structure with creativity, and tradition with transformation? The future of teaching demands that you go beyond the blackboard and step into a world where learning is dynamic, immersive, and deeply personal.

This section is designed to challenge your thinking and expand your approach to teaching. It explores some of the most pressing questions in modern education—Should attendance be redefined? Is homework still effective? Does penmanship still matter in a digital age? It provides research-backed strategies to help you navigate these complexities, ensuring that your classroom becomes more than just a space for instruction—it becomes a hub of exploration, discovery, and inspiration.

Chapter 16
Rethinking Attendance

Attendance is more than just presence—it's about engagement, curiosity, and creating a classroom where students want to show up and truly learn.

For years, attendance has been treated as a measure of discipline—a box to be checked rather than a reflection of meaningful learning. However, as you know, simply having students in the classroom does not guarantee engagement. Some may be physically present but mentally elsewhere, distracted or disinterested. Others may struggle with attendance due to anxiety, disengagement, or external pressures beyond their control. The real question is: Are students showing up because they have to or because they want to?

As a teacher, you have the power to transform attendance from an obligation into an opportunity. Instead of enforcing presence, imagine making learning so compelling that students *choose* to be there. When your students feel seen, supported, and inspired—when they recognize the value of their education—attendance naturally follows. The challenge, then, isn't just ensuring students are present; it's making them feel that their presence matters.

Attendance is not just about following school policies—it's about you ensuring that your students receive the education, guidance, and encouragement they need to grow intellectually, emotionally, and socially. While consistent attendance is linked to academic success, it also fosters relationships, critical thinking, and essential life skills. Your role is more than taking roll—it's about creating an environment where every student feels engaged, valued, and motivated to participate, not just physically but mentally and emotionally.

When students frequently miss school, they lose more than just lessons. They miss your guidance, class discussions, peer collaboration, and the deeper connections that make learning meaningful. These gaps weaken their relationship with education and make re-engagement even harder. That's why understanding the reasons behind student absences is just as important as tracking them.

Attendance should not be about compliance—it should be about connection. When you design your lessons to be interactive, relevant, and inspiring, students won't just show up out of duty—they'll show up because they want to. What can you do to make your classroom the kind of place where students wouldn't dream of missing a single day?

Why Do Students Skip Class?

But first, let's explore the question: **Why Do Students Skip Class?** Could it be that learning in your classroom feels more like a routine task than an inspiring journey? Is learning truly engaging, or has it become insipid and disconnected from what excites and motivates your students?

Absenteeism is often treated as a discipline issue, but what if it's a symptom of deeper challenges within the education system? As a teacher, you are not just an enforcer of attendance—you are the bridge between a student and their sense of purpose in learning. The question isn't just *"Why do students skip class?"* but rather, *"What does their absence reveal about the learning environment, their personal struggles, and the gaps in our educational approach?"* If your students don't find a subject meaningful, they will naturally disengage. But disengagement isn't just about boredom—it's about a failure to see relevance.

When learning feels like a passive exercise in memorization rather than a dynamic exploration of ideas, students mentally and physically check out. Are your students co-creators in their learning, or are they merely passive receivers of information? Do they see how your lessons connect to their real-world aspirations, challenges, and future careers? Are you teaching students, or are you just teaching content? A disengaged student skipping your class isn't rebelling against education—they are rejecting an approach that doesn't speak to them. The challenge lies in transforming education from a compulsory routine into a compelling experience. You can make that difference. When you incorporate active, inquiry-based learning, hands-on projects, and student-driven discussions, you make learning feel relevant. And when students find meaning in what they are learning, your struggle with attendance won't be about enforcement—it will become a natural consequence of their genuine engagement.

Do You Encourage Growth or Just Performance?

For some students, skipping your class isn't an act of defiance—it's a defence mechanism. It's a way to avoid exposure, embarrassment, or the crushing pressure of perfectionism. If your classroom culture prioritizes correctness over curiosity, students may retreat rather than risk being wrong. Is failure in your class treated as part of learning or as a mark against a student's intelligence? Do your students feel comfortable asking questions, making mistakes, and experimenting with ideas? Is participation seen as an opportunity for growth or as a performance to be judged? Students who fear judgment often choose invisibility. It's not about their capability—it's about their psychological safety. Your classroom can be a place where students feel safe to take risks, challenge ideas, and grow without fear. A truly engaging class isn't just intellectually stimulating—it's emotionally secure. When you create an environment where students know that their voices matter, their ideas are valued, and mistakes are stepping stones to understanding, you encourage not just attendance but genuine investment in learning.

Is Your Classroom a Safe Space or a Stress Space?

Not all absences are about academics. Sometimes, a student skips your class because it's easier than confronting bullying, loneliness, or a lack of belonging. You might work in a school with strict anti-bullying policies, but do your students feel emotionally protected, included, and valued? Are there cliques, silent exclusions, or social hierarchies that make some students feel like outsiders? Do all your students see themselves reflected in the curriculum, classroom discussions, and leadership opportunities? Are you fostering a culture of inclusion or simply enforcing compliance with rules? An emotionally disconnected student will disengage long before they physically stop showing up. Attendance isn't just about physical presence; it's about psychological presence. You have the power to build a sense of community and belonging. Your efforts to foster collaboration, encourage peer connections, and create an inclusive classroom culture can make all the difference. When your students feel valued and supported, they are far more likely to engage and attend consistently.

Do You See the Student Beyond the Classroom?

Some absences have nothing to do with your classroom or even the school itself. Your students may be carrying invisible burdens—family struggles, financial hardship, mental health challenges, or personal crises. Instead of asking, *"Why aren't they showing up?"*, ask yourself, *"What are they dealing with outside these walls?"*

As a teacher, you may not be able to fix these challenges, but you can create flexible learning options for students facing real-life struggles. Are you checking in with students who miss class—not as an act of discipline, but as an act of care? A simple conversation, a message, or an offer of support can make a profound difference.

You have the power to advocate for mental health support and student well-being initiatives that go beyond academics. Ignoring these challenges won't make them disappear—it will only make your students disappear from your classroom.

By offering support, creating alternative ways for students to engage, and recognizing the complexities of their lives, you can help them navigate their struggles while staying connected to their education. Your role is more than just teaching—it's about seeing, understanding, and empowering every student who walks through your door.

Beyond Attendance

When students skip class, they aren't just making a choice—they are sending a message. The real challenge is whether we are listening. Attendance is not just about monitoring presence; it's about cultivating a space where students actually want to be present—physically, emotionally, and intellectually.

So, the next time a student is absent, ask not just *why*—but *what needs to change in our approach to learning to bring them back?* When students feel connected, valued, and engaged, attendance becomes a natural outcome rather than a forced obligation. Here are some effective strategies to encourage attendance through engagement.

Make Learning Meaningful and Interactive: A dry, lecture-heavy approach can sap enthusiasm from even the most curious minds. Instead, you can create a more engaging learning experience by making lessons interactive and relevant. Use real-world applications and problem-solving activities to help students connect what they are learning to their daily lives. Incorporate hands-on projects, debates, role-playing, and gamification to make subjects more dynamic and exciting. Leverage technology and multimedia tools to cater to different learning styles, ensuring that all students remain engaged. When students see the value in their education, they are more likely to invest in learning and attend class regularly.

Personalize Learning Experiences: Every student has unique interests, strengths, and challenges. A one-size-fits-all approach can make some students feel disconnected from the material. Instead, offer students choices in how they demonstrate their learning—whether through presentations, creative projects, or research. Find ways to link lessons to their passions, whether it be music, sports, technology, or storytelling. Provide flexible learning pathways, including self-paced or inquiry-based learning, to accommodate diverse learning styles. When students feel a sense of ownership over their education, they are more motivated to show up and participate actively.

Foster Strong Teacher-Student Relationships: Students are more likely to attend class when they feel valued, respected, and understood by you. Take the time to greet students warmly and show a genuine interest in their well-being. Create a classroom culture where mistakes are seen as learning opportunities rather than failures. Check in with students who seem withdrawn or absent, letting them know that they are missed and supported. A simple conversation, an encouraging note, or even recognizing a student's effort can make a significant difference in their decision to attend class. When students know that you care about them beyond just their grades, they are more likely to engage in learning.

Create a Positive and Inclusive Classroom Culture: Your classroom should feel like a safe and inspiring space, not just a place of rules and expectations. Encourage collaboration rather than competition—group projects, peer mentoring, and team-based learning can create a sense of belonging among students. Promote a growth mindset by celebrating effort and progress just as much as achievement. Make room for humor, creativity, and moments of joy; learning should be enjoyable, not just another task. When students feel comfortable and included in your classroom, they are more likely to attend and engage meaningfully.

Recognize and Celebrate Attendance and Engagement: Rather than focusing on punishing absences, shift the emphasis to recognizing and rewarding student effort. Celebrate small wins by acknowledging students who show improvement in participation and attendance. Offer meaningful incentives such as leadership opportunities, public recognition, or student-led activities. Encourage peer encouragement—when students support each other, they contribute to a positive learning environment. Recognition doesn't have to be extravagant—even a simple *"Great to see you today!"* can reinforce the importance of attending and participating in class.

Turn Attendance into a Choice, Not a Chore: Rethinking attendance isn't about ignoring its importance—it's about redefining its purpose. When students want to be in your classroom because they find learning meaningful, relevant, and enjoyable, attendance takes care of itself. As a teacher, you are a source of inspiration. Your passion, creativity, and connection with students have the power to make education more than just a requirement; you can make it a journey of discovery, curiosity, and lifelong learning.

Attendance should never be about compliance—it should be about belonging.

Chapter 17
The Homework Debate

Homework isn't about more or less—it's about balance. Too much overwhelms, and too little hinders growth. The right amount fosters learning, creativity, and rest.

Is Homework a Valuable Learning Tool or Just Another Stress Factor?

For generations, homework has been an unquestioned part of education, a bridge between classroom learning and independent study. But as an educator, you must ask yourself: Are you assigning homework to enhance learning, or are you simply following tradition? The debate over homework is not about eliminating it altogether but about striking the right balance—ensuring that assignments contribute meaningfully to your students' academic growth without leading to stress, disengagement, or burnout.

Why Homework?

At its core, homework serves several purposes. It reinforces classroom learning, helping your students solidify concepts taught in class through independent practice. Beyond academics, it develops essential study habits, encouraging discipline, time management, and self-directed learning—skills that extend beyond the classroom. Additionally, homework fosters parental involvement by allowing parents to engage with their child's education and track academic progress. Another significant role of homework is in preparing students for future lessons; assignments can act as a primer for upcoming topics, enabling learners to enter the classroom with background knowledge.

However, simply assigning homework does not guarantee these benefits. The quality of assignments matters more than the quantity. Well-planned, purposeful homework enriches learning, while excessive, repetitive tasks can have the opposite effect.

The Benefits of Homework - When Done Right

Homework, when assigned strategically, can have a profound impact on your students' academic success. One of its greatest advantages is its role in enhancing retention. Well-designed assignments reinforce what has been taught in class, helping students retain information better. Another major benefit is that it encourages critical thinking. Thought-provoking tasks, rather than repetitive exercises, foster analytical skills and problem-solving abilities, which are essential for higher-order learning.

Personalized learning is another advantage of homework. When students are given a choice—such as project-based work, presentations, or creative tasks—they gain autonomy in exploring subjects in ways that interest them. This sense of ownership enhances motivation and engagement. Additionally, homework can serve as a bridge between classroom and real-world learning. Practical, application-based assignments connect academic theories with everyday experiences, making learning more relevant and meaningful.

The Negative Effects of Excessive Homework

While homework has clear benefits, too much of it can be counterproductive. Research suggests that an excessive workload can lead to increased stress and anxiety. When your students are overwhelmed with assignments, they experience pressure that reduces their enthusiasm for learning and negatively affects their mental health. Furthermore, excessive homework consumes valuable family and leisure time. Overburdened students miss out on crucial family bonding, play, and relaxation—activities essential for holistic development.

Another major drawback of excessive homework is its impact on engagement and motivation. When your students associate homework with stress rather than learning, their motivation declines. This often results in incomplete assignments, reduced classroom participation, and a loss of interest in education. Additionally, an overwhelming amount of homework can contribute to burnout and sleep deprivation. Many students sacrifice sleep to complete assignments, which negatively impacts their focus, memory, and overall academic performance.

The key takeaway is that more homework does not necessarily mean better learning. Your goal should be to assign homework that is meaningful, manageable, and motivating rather than burdensome.

How Much Homework is Enough?

The question of how much homework is appropriate has long been debated among educators, parents, and policymakers. While some argue that homework is necessary for reinforcing classroom learning, others point out that excessive assignments can lead to stress, burnout, and disengagement. Striking the right balance is crucial to ensuring that homework serves as an effective learning tool rather than a source of unnecessary pressure.

One of the most widely accepted frameworks for determining appropriate homework duration is the "10-Minute Rule," a guideline introduced by educational researcher Harris Cooper. This principle suggests that students should be assigned homework in increments of 10 minutes per grade level per night. For instance:

- ✓ Grade 1 → 10 minutes

- ✓ Grade 2 → 20 minutes

- ✓ Grade 3 → 30 minutes

- ✓ … and so on, with a maximum of 120 minutes (2 hours) for 12th-grade students.

This model helps maintain a balance between academic rigor and student well-being by preventing an overwhelming workload. Many schools worldwide have adopted this approach to ensure that students are given adequate time for extracurricular activities, social interactions, rest, and personal interests. Research supports this model, indicating that moderate, purposeful homework improves learning outcomes, while excessive assignments diminish their effectiveness and can lead to negative consequences such as anxiety, lack of motivation, and reduced family time.

However, simply following a numerical rule is not enough. The quality of homework matters just as much as its quantity. As a teacher, you must carefully design assignments to reinforce classroom learning, encourage independent thinking, and provide opportunities for creative expression. Consider the diverse needs of your students, ensuring that homework is inclusive and does not disadvantage those with limited access to resources at home.

What Does the Education Policy Say About Homework?

As a teacher, you play a crucial role in shaping your students' learning experiences. While homework is an essential tool for reinforcing concepts, excessive assignments can overwhelm students, leaving little room for creativity, play, and personal growth. Recognizing this, India's School Bag Policy, 2020, issued by the National Council of Educational Research and Training (NCERT), provides clear guidelines on how much homework students should receive at different grade levels.

Homework Guidelines Under the School Bag Policy, 2020

To ensure a balanced approach, the policy recommends:

- ✓ Classes 1-2: No homework.

- ✓ Classes 3-5: A maximum of two hours per week.

- ✓ Classes 6-8: A maximum of one hour per day.

- ✓ Classes 9-12: A maximum of two hours per day.

As a teacher, these guidelines offer an opportunity for you to rethink the way you design homework. Instead of assigning repetitive tasks that add little value to a student's understanding, consider how homework can be used as a meaningful extension of classroom learning. The policy encourages you to focus on designing assignments that engage students in problem-solving, creativity, and real-world applications.

By shifting towards quality over quantity, you can make homework a valuable tool for student growth. Instead of long, tedious exercises, consider incorporating project-based assignments, problem-solving tasks, and creative exercises such as storytelling, research projects, or hands-on experiments. These types of assignments not only reinforce learning but also make the process more enjoyable and engaging for your students.

Rethinking Homework Practices

As a teacher, it is essential to reflect on the true purpose and impact of homework. Assigning more work does not necessarily lead to better learning outcomes. Instead, homework should be thoughtfully structured to reinforce classroom learning, foster creativity, and encourage independent exploration.

Here are some best practices to ensure that assignments remain effective, engaging, and purposeful:

- ✓ Every homework assignment should have a clear learning objective, reinforcing classroom concepts rather than being assigned for the sake of completion.

- ✓ Give students autonomy in how they complete their assignments.

- ✓ A well-designed, concise assignment is more effective than a long, monotonous task based on rote memorization.

- ✓ Assignments that involve peer discussions, group projects, or family interactions make learning more dynamic.

- ✓ Relating tasks to students' experiences, interests, and real-world applications enhances understanding.

As a teacher, you hold the key to shaping homework practices that empower rather than burden students. The goal is not just to assign work but to inspire lifelong learning, ensuring that homework becomes a tool for growth rather than a source of stress.

Chapter 18
Does Penmanship Still Matter?

Handwriting isn't just words on paper—it's the art of thought, the rhythm of focus, and the mark of individuality. In a digital world, your pen still holds power!

With the rapid rise of digital technology, the way you and your students write and communicate has drastically changed. Typing has become the dominant mode of writing, replacing pen and paper in classrooms, workplaces, and personal communication. As digital devices become more accessible, you may question whether handwriting is still relevant in the modern world. Some argue that learning to type efficiently is far more valuable than mastering penmanship, given that most professional and academic tasks now require digital literacy.

However, studies in neuroscience and education suggest that handwriting plays a crucial role in cognitive development, learning, and creativity. Writing by hand is more than just a motor skill; it engages multiple areas of the brain and strengthens neural pathways that contribute to memory retention, comprehension, and focus. Despite the convenience of typing, there are compelling reasons why you should not abandon handwriting in your teaching. Instead of viewing handwriting and typing as opposing skills, you can explore how both can be integrated to maximize cognitive and creative benefits for your students.

The Science Behind Handwriting

Why does handwriting still matter in your classroom? In today's digital age, you may wonder if handwriting still holds a place in your classroom. However, studies continue to show that writing by hand plays a crucial role in learning and cognitive development. Beyond simply putting words on paper, handwriting engages multiple areas of the brain, strengthens memory, and enhances critical thinking skills. As an educator, understanding the science behind handwriting can help you create a more effective and engaging learning environment for your students.

Handwriting Enhances Your Students' Memory Retention: Scientific studies have shown that handwriting significantly improves memory retention compared to typing. When students write by hand, they engage the sensorimotor system, activating different regions of the brain, including the prefrontal cortex, motor cortex, and hippocampus—areas responsible for learning and memory formation. A landmark study by Mueller and Oppenheimer (2014) compared students who took notes by hand versus those who typed their notes on a laptop. The results showed that students who wrote by hand retained information more effectively and performed better on conceptual questions. The reason? Handwriting requires deeper processing of information, as students summarize key points rather than transcribing word-for-word as they do when typing. This cognitive effort strengthens memory encoding and improves recall ability.

Writing by Hand Improves Focus and Engagement in Your Lessons: Typing is a faster method of recording information, but its speed can sometimes lead to passive engagement with content. Many students who type their notes tend to multitask, switch between applications, or copy text without fully processing it. On the other hand, handwriting forces them to slow down, filter essential information, and engage in active learning. When writing by hand, the brain's reticular activating system (RAS) is stimulated, enhancing focus and attention. The act of forming letters and structuring sentences requires more cognitive effort, leading to deeper comprehension. This is particularly important in your classroom, where critical thinking and understanding play a crucial role in learning outcomes.

Handwriting Fosters Creativity and Ideation in Your Students: Handwriting has been linked to enhanced creativity, as the physical act of writing encourages free-flowing thoughts and idea generation. Research suggests that when students write by hand, their brains exhibit increased activity in the left fusiform gyrus, an area associated with creative thinking and visual recognition. Many writers, artists, and thinkers—such as J.K. Rowling, Albert Einstein, and Leonardo da Vinci—preferred handwriting for brainstorming and developing ideas. The fluidity of cursive writing, in particular, allows thoughts to flow more naturally compared to typing, which can sometimes feel rigid and disconnected. Encouraging students to write by hand during brainstorming sessions can help them develop stronger and more original ideas.

Handwriting Fosters Cognitive and Motor Development: For young learners, handwriting is an essential skill that aids in fine motor development and neural coordination. Studies have shown that children who practice handwriting develop stronger hand-eye coordination, spatial awareness, and dexterity compared to those who rely primarily on typing. Furthermore, learning to write by hand reinforces letter recognition, spelling, and reading skills. The "dual coding theory" suggests that when children learn to write letters manually, they create stronger mental associations between the shape, sound, and meaning of words. This contributes to better literacy skills and language development in early childhood education.

Integrating Both Handwriting and Typing in Your Teaching

While handwriting has significant cognitive advantages, you also recognize that typing is an essential skill in today's world. In professional and academic settings, the ability to type quickly and accurately is crucial for productivity and efficiency. Typing allows students to record large amounts of information rapidly, collaborate in real time, and access digital tools that enhance learning and communication. For students with disabilities or motor impairments, typing and speech-to-text technologies provide accessibility and ease of communication. Additionally, in careers that require extensive documentation, coding, or online collaboration, typing is often the preferred mode of writing. However, the reliance on typing has also led to concerns such as digital distractions, reduced handwriting abilities, and superficial processing of information. Striking a balance between handwriting and typing is key to developing a well-rounded approach to writing and learning in your classroom.

So, rather than choosing between handwriting and typing, you can combine both methods to enhance learning, retention, and creative expression. Here are some strategies to find the right balance:

✓ Allow students to use a mix of handwritten and typed notes depending on the subject and task. For instance, handwritten notes can be useful for brainstorming, summarizing, and concept mapping, while digital notes can be used for research and collaboration.

✓ Providing students with the flexibility to choose between handwriting and typing based on their learning preferences can lead to greater engagement. Some may prefer handwritten notes for studying and revision, while others may find digital tools more efficient for drafting and editing.

✓ Encouraging students to engage in handwriting exercises—such as journaling, freewriting, and diagramming—can improve cognitive function and creative thinking. Mind-mapping and sketching ideas by hand often lead to deeper insights and problem-solving abilities.

✓ With the advancement of stylus technology and digital notebooks, students can now experience the benefits of handwriting while maintaining the convenience of digital storage. Apps like OneNote, Notability, and Good Notes allow users to write by hand on tablets while still organizing their notes digitally.

While technology has transformed how your students write and communicate, handwriting remains a vital skill that offers numerous cognitive, creative, and developmental benefits. Rather than viewing handwriting as an outdated practice, you can embrace a hybrid approach that integrates both handwriting and typing. Handwriting enhances memory, improves focus, and fosters creativity, while typing enhances efficiency, collaboration, and accessibility. By striking a balance between the two, you can help your students develop stronger literacy skills, critical thinking abilities, and a deeper engagement with learning.

Chapter 19
More Than Just Fabric

A uniform is more than just fabric—it weaves together discipline, unity, and pride.

Uniforms have been a longstanding tradition in schools, workplaces, and organizations worldwide. While some may see them as merely a dress code requirement, uniforms serve a much deeper purpose. They instil discipline, foster unity, and create an environment conducive to learning and professionalism. The history of uniforms dates back centuries, with roots in military, religious, and educational settings. But why were they introduced in schools? And how do they impact personality development? This chapter explores the psychological reasoning behind school uniforms, their first recorded use, and their profound influence on individuals.

The first known use of school uniforms can be traced back to 16th-century England, where Christ's Hospital School in London introduced a standard dress code for its students. The primary purpose was to create a sense of discipline and equality, ensuring that all children, regardless of their socio-economic backgrounds, had access to the same educational experience.

In the 19th and 20th centuries, uniforms became more common in schools across Europe, Asia, and America. Many private and public schools worldwide later adopted uniforms to maintain order, reduce distractions, and create a focused learning environment.

As a teacher, understanding the significance of uniforms beyond just fabric helps you appreciate their role in shaping your students' behaviour, discipline, and identity. By recognizing these deeper implications, you can guide your students more effectively and create an environment that promotes holistic growth.

The Psychology and Purpose Behind School Uniforms

The implementation of uniforms is not just a cultural or traditional practice—it is backed by psychology and social science. Research suggests that wearing a uniform influences an individual's behaviour, confidence, and social interactions in several key ways:

Uniforms Reduce Decision Fatigue – Psychologists argue that wearing a uniform minimizes the mental burden of deciding what to wear each day, allowing students and professionals to focus their cognitive energy on more important tasks. This principle is evident in high-achieving individuals like Steve Jobs and Mark Zuckerberg, who wore the same type of clothing daily to eliminate unnecessary decisions.

Uniforms Promote Equality – By removing visible economic differences, uniforms create a sense of social cohesion. Without the pressure to wear trendy or expensive clothing, students can concentrate on their studies rather than social status.

Uniforms Enhance Discipline and Structure – Behavioural studies indicate that wearing a uniform subconsciously reinforces discipline, as students associate the attire with a structured environment where learning is the priority.

Uniforms Strengthen Identity and Belonging – Wearing a uniform foster a stronger connection to one's school or institution. This sense of belonging instils pride, responsibility, and motivation, enhancing both engagement and performance.

As teachers, understanding these psychological effects allows you to reinforce the values that uniforms promote. By helping students see uniforms as more than just clothing, you can guide them in developing positive associations with discipline, structure, and self-respect.

Uniforms and Personality Development

Wearing a uniform does not just affect external behaviour; it plays a crucial role in shaping personality and self-perception. The way your students present themselves in a structured dress code influences their confidence, mindset, and interpersonal interactions.

Boosts Confidence and Self-Esteem – Studies show that when individuals wear uniforms, they experience a psychological shift in self-perception. Your students may feel more responsible, focused, and professional in their attire.

Enhances Group Identity and Team Spirit – Uniforms create a shared identity among students, fostering unity and reducing conflicts related to fashion-based social divisions. This promotes teamwork and collaboration in your classroom.

Encourages Professionalism and Preparedness – By dressing in a uniform, students develop habits that prepare them for future workplace expectations, reinforcing traits like punctuality, orderliness, and responsibility.

Develops a Sense of Respect and Pride – Uniforms symbolize affiliation with an institution, helping your students feel a sense of honor and duty toward upholding the values of their school or organization.

As a teacher, you play a vital role in helping your students understand how uniforms shape their self-perception. By fostering a positive perspective, you can encourage them to embrace their attire with confidence and pride, seeing it as a symbol of unity and identity rather than a restriction.

Debates surrounding uniforms

The debate over school uniforms continues to spark discussions on the balance between unity and individuality. As teachers, it is crucial to recognize that while uniforms promote equality by eliminating socio-economic disparities, fostering discipline, and reducing distractions, they may also feel restrictive to students who seek self-expression. Supporters argue that a standardized dress code enhances school spirit and creates a focused learning environment, while critics emphasize the importance of personal choice, comfort, and cultural diversity. Rather than viewing this as a rigid issue, teachers can approach it as an opportunity to instill in students the understanding that identity is shaped by values, integrity, and aspirations rather than attire. By fostering an environment where students take pride in who they are—whether in uniform or not—teachers can help them develop confidence, resilience, and a sense of belonging. Additionally, advocating for flexible and inclusive uniform policies can strike a balance between structure and self-expression, ensuring that the benefits of school uniforms align with the evolving needs of students.

As a teacher, you have a wonderful opportunity to help students see that school uniforms are more than just fabric—they serve as a means of fostering discipline, equality, and a sense of belonging. While some students may initially feel that uniforms limit their choices, they play an important role in shaping behaviour, reducing socio-economic differences, and creating a focused learning environment. A well-structured dress code can also promote school spirit, minimize distractions, and encourage professionalism—qualities that will support students in their academic journey and beyond.

At the same time, it's essential to acknowledge that students value self-expression and individuality. Some may feel that uniforms restrict their ability to express their personality, and rigid dress codes may not always accommodate cultural diversity or practical considerations. Rather than dismissing these concerns, you can turn them into meaningful discussions, helping students reflect on how identity is shaped not just by clothing but by values, integrity, and aspirations.

Instead of seeing the debate over uniforms as a matter of strict enforcement, you can advocate for thoughtful and inclusive policies that maintain discipline while allowing reasonable flexibility. By fostering an environment where students feel a sense of pride in who they are—whether in uniform or not—you help them develop confidence, resilience, and a deeper understanding of unity and respect. Your role extends beyond enforcing rules; it is about inspiring students to appreciate the values behind those rules and guiding them toward a balanced perspective on individuality and belonging.

Chapter 20
Beyond The Bell

Learning doesn't stop when the bell rings—it begins. Beyond the bell lies curiosity, growth, and the endless pursuit of knowledge.

Imagine walking into your classroom and witnessing two vastly different scenarios. In one, students are scattered, unsure of what to do next, their attention drifting aimlessly. In the other, students transition seamlessly between tasks, fully aware of expectations, engaged and focused. The difference? A well-structured class routine.

A class routine is not merely a schedule—it is the invisible framework that cultivates a thriving learning environment. It fosters discipline, enhances focus, and establishes a predictable yet dynamic space where students can flourish. For Generation Z (born 1997–2012) and Generation Alpha (born 2013–present), structure plays a pivotal role in shaping cognitive, emotional, and social development. In a world dominated by digital distractions, a well-planned routine serves as an anchor, providing stability while fostering creativity and flexibility.

A thoughtfully designed routine does more than streamline classroom management; it strengthens students' ability to learn, builds self-discipline, and fosters a sense of security. As an educator, you are not merely managing time—you are shaping experiences that have a profound impact on students' academic success and personal growth.

The Science Behind Structure

"Structure is not about control; it's about setting students up for success."

– Harry K. Wong

Students' brains are constantly processing an overwhelming amount of information. Cognitive Load Theory (Sweller, 1988) explains that when students face too many unpredictable elements, their working memory becomes overwhelmed, making learning inefficient. A structured routine reduces this cognitive load by minimizing decision fatigue, allowing students to focus their mental energy on grasping new concepts rather than worrying about what happens next. A predictable classroom rhythm—such as beginning with a warm-up, transitioning into instruction, followed by group work, and concluding with reflection—creates a sense of security. Students are more engaged when they do not have to second-guess their next steps, freeing up mental resources for deeper learning.

Additionally, research on memory, particularly Ebbinghaus's Forgetting Curve (1885), highlights the importance of reinforcement. Without periodic review, students forget nearly half of what they learn within hours. However, when information is revisited at strategic intervals, retention improves significantly. Incorporating review sessions, interactive discussions, and reflective exercises into your daily routine strengthens memory retention. It encourages students to actively engage with the material rather than passively absorb information, fostering deeper understanding and long-term recall.

Routine and Responsibility

"The best way to develop responsibility in students is to give them responsibilities."

– Fred Jones

Beyond academics, structured routines play a critical role in shaping responsible individuals. B.F. Skinner's Operant Conditioning (1953) suggests that structured routines reinforce positive behaviours, helping students develop self-discipline and time management skills. When students know what is expected of them—whether it is completing assignments, organizing materials, or participating in discussions—they become more accountable for their learning. A consistent schedule trains students to meet deadlines, manage their time efficiently, and take initiative—skills essential for future success in higher education and professional life.

Emotional Security and Engagement

"Students thrive in an environment where expectations are clear and consistent."

– Carol Ann Tomlinson

A predictable routine fosters an emotionally secure environment, particularly for students struggling with anxiety or learning difficulties. Research by Pianta et al. (2008) suggests that structured environments strengthen teacher-student relationships, leading to higher engagement and academic achievement. When students know what to expect, they feel more confident, willing to participate, and less anxious. Integrating short movement breaks, mindfulness exercises, or creative activities within your routine can further enhance energy levels and sustain motivation. Striking a balance between structure and flexibility ensures that all students—regardless of their learning styles—feel comfortable, engaged, and supported.

Beyond the Classroom

"Good teaching is one-fourth preparation and three-fourths theatre."

– Gail Godwin

A well-structured class routine is not about imposing rigid rules—it is about creating a foundation for meaningful learning experiences. Your efforts in designing and maintaining an effective routine will not only benefit students in the present but also equip them with habits of discipline, focus, and responsibility that will shape their futures. By fostering a classroom culture of predictability and engagement, you are doing more than just delivering lessons—you are preparing students for a lifetime of learning and success.

So, as you plan your days, remember: every routine you establish, every transition you refine, and every expectation you set extends far beyond the classroom walls. It shapes young minds beyond the bell, instilling lifelong skills that will guide them long after they have left your care.

Rethinking Class Periods for Maximum Impact

"The best teachers are those who show you where to look but don't tell you what to see."

– Alexandra K. Trenfor

One of the most pressing questions teachers face is how to structure the school day effectively. How many periods should there be? How long should they last? The answer lies not just in the number of periods but in how time is utilized within them. A well-balanced school schedule considers cognitive load, student engagement, and real-world applicability. It ensures that students not only absorb information but also develop the ability to think critically, solve problems, and apply their learning in meaningful ways.

In elementary schools, where younger students have shorter attention spans, 5-6 shorter periods are ideal. These periods blend structured learning with play, allowing children to stay engaged while building foundational skills. Shorter sessions also cater to their natural curiosity and need for movement, ensuring that learning remains interactive and enjoyable.

For high school students, 6-8 periods work best as they allow for deeper subject exploration and college or career preparation. As students mature, they require longer periods to develop critical thinking, engage in discussions, and apply concepts in practical settings. A well-planned schedule balances core subjects, electives, and enrichment activities, ensuring a holistic educational experience.

For Generation Z (born 1997-2012) and Generation Alpha (born 2013- present), traditional class structures may no longer be as effective. These students thrive in hybrid learning models that incorporate digital tools, problem-solving activities, and flexible schedules. They benefit from interactive, tech-enhanced lessons that make learning dynamic and relevant to the digital era. Regardless of the number of periods, the most crucial factor is how classroom time is used. Movement breaks, creative sessions, and reflection periods are essential in making learning more effective and engaging. By designing schedules that prioritize both structure and flexibility, teachers can create an environment that fosters curiosity, motivation, and lifelong learning.

Designing the Perfect Class Routine

As a teacher, you know that a well-structured class routine is more than just a schedule—it is the foundation for meaningful learning. A thoughtfully designed routine helps you maximize engagement while fostering discipline, creativity, and student autonomy. The challenge is to balance structure with flexibility, ensuring that your students remain focused while also giving them opportunities to explore and connect with the material.

To create a high-impact class routine that works across different learning styles, you can incorporate the following elements:

Setting the Tone for Learning: The beginning of your class sets the stage for the entire lesson. Instead of jumping straight into the subject matter, consider starting with a short, interactive activity that grabs students' attention. This could include a quick journaling prompt, a thought-provoking question, or a brief mindfulness exercise to help students settle in. By doing this, you help students transition from the distractions of their day into a focused mindset for learning.

Delivering Core Concepts: This is the heart of your lesson, where you introduce key ideas, theories, or skills. However, instead of relying solely on traditional lectures, try incorporating a variety of teaching methods to keep your students engaged. You might use storytelling, real-world applications, engaging videos, or inquiry-based learning to make the content more relatable and thought-provoking. When you make your lessons interactive and relevant, you deepen students' understanding and make learning more enjoyable.

Bringing Learning to Life: Students learn best when they are actively involved. After introducing new concepts, give your students the opportunity to engage with the material through hands-on activities, group discussions, or problem-solving exercises. This phase encourages collaboration, critical thinking, and real-world application of knowledge. By allowing students to interact with each other and with the content in meaningful ways, you create an environment where learning becomes a dynamic and personal experience.

Review and Reflection: Learning is most effective when students have time to process and reflect. At the end of your lesson, encourage your students to summarize what they've learned through guided discussions, Q&A sessions, or self-assessments. Reflection helps solidify knowledge and allows students to see the connections between what they have learned and how they can apply it in the future. You might ask open-ended questions, such as:

- ✓ What was the most interesting thing you learned today?

- ✓ How can you apply today's lesson to your daily life?

- ✓ What questions do you still have?

A teacher once shared, *"I used to dive straight into my lessons and rush to finish everything, but when I started adding moments for mindfulness and reflection, I noticed a real difference in my students' engagement and understanding. Sometimes, a five-minute pause makes all the difference."*

Creative/Physical Break: A well-structured class routine isn't just about academic learning—it should also incorporate moments for creativity and movement. Short breaks, such as a quick stretching session, listening to music, or engaging in a hands-on creative activity, help re-energize students and improve focus. This is especially important in today's digital age, where students spend long hours in front of screens. By incorporating movement and creativity into your lessons, you foster a classroom environment that supports both cognitive and emotional well-being.

Teaching with Purpose

As a teacher, your goal is not just to fill a class period with content but to create an environment where learning is meaningful, engaging, and transformative. Great teaching is not about rigid schedules; it's about understanding your students, meeting their needs, and guiding them toward success. No matter what subject you teach or what grade level you work with, your ability to design and adapt class routines plays a critical role in shaping students' experiences.

Here are three principles to keep in mind:

Be adaptable – Education is evolving, and so should your teaching methods. Embrace new strategies and technologies that enhance learning.

Be intentional – Every period should serve a purpose beyond just covering the syllabus. Make each lesson meaningful by connecting it to real-life applications.

Be inspiring – Your passion, energy, and creativity will leave a lasting impact on your students. When you bring enthusiasm into your teaching, your students will be more motivated to learn.

"A great teacher is one who not only teaches but also inspires a love for learning."

As education continues to evolve, so must class routines. The rigid schedules of the past are giving way to dynamic, student-centered learning models that emphasize flexibility, innovation, and adaptability. A well-structured routine is not about control—it is about creating a space where students feel confident, engaged, and inspired to reach their full potential.

By embracing structured yet adaptable class schedules, you empower your students to develop self-discipline, think critically, and become lifelong learners. Teaching goes beyond delivering content; it is about shaping habits, fostering curiosity, and preparing students for success in an ever-changing world.

So, what's one small change you can make in your class routine today to spark more curiosity and joy in your students? Let's go beyond the bell and make classrooms places where learning flows seamlessly, igniting curiosity and growth in every student.

* * *

Section V
Professional Mastery

(Empowering teachers with Essential skills for growth, balance, and success in teaching.)

Professional Mastery

Professional mastery for teachers is not just about expertise—it's a commitment to lifelong learning, innovation, and inspiring growth in every student.

As a teacher, mastering your profession means actively seeking professional development, staying updated with innovative teaching methodologies, and adapting to the diverse needs of your students. Whether it's integrating AI, enhancing engagement strategies, or fostering deeper learning experiences, your ability to evolve determines your effectiveness.

But professional mastery is not just about learning new strategies—it's about your self-reflection and adaptability. Evaluating your teaching methods, embracing feedback, and modifying approaches help create meaningful learning experiences. Your strong relationships with students, your open communication with parents, and your collaboration with colleagues further amplify your impact. Teaching is not a solitary journey—it thrives on your mentorship, shared insights, and a culture of collective growth.

Beyond the classroom, your professional mastery extends to career growth, financial stability, and personal well-being. Planning for your long-term success, achieving your work-life balance, and ensuring your financial security are just as essential as lesson planning. A fulfilled and motivated teacher—like you—radiates inspiration, encouraging students to learn, dream, and grow.

And one day, when you retire, your legacy will live on—not in lesson plans, but in the minds you've shaped and the lives you've transformed. Your journey as a teacher never truly ends. Professional mastery ensures that you leave a mark that lasts for generations.

Let's dive into the journey of **Professional Mastery**—where growth never stops, impact never fades, and your legacy begins!

Chapter 21
Harnessing The Power Of Feedback

Feedback is not criticism; it's a compass for growth. Teachers who embrace it see every insight as an opportunity to refine, inspire, and elevate their impact.

Imagine a musician who never listens to an audience's reaction or a chef who never tastes their own food. Teaching is no different. The best teachers refine their craft through continuous learning and adaptation. However, many teachers hesitate when faced with feedback, often misinterpreting it as criticism rather than a powerful tool for improvement.

Great teaching is not about perfection—it is about progress. Each day in the classroom presents an opportunity to grow, but that growth can only happen when you embrace feedback with an open mind and a willingness to evolve. In this chapter, you will discover how to shift your mindset, identify valuable sources of feedback, and transform insights into meaningful action that enhances both your teaching and your students' learning experiences.

Many teachers perceive feedback as an attack rather than an opportunity, but your key to professional growth lies in shifting from a defensive stance to a growth-oriented mindset. How you perceive feedback can directly impact your improvement and success in the classroom. Instead of seeing it as criticism, embrace it as a tool for your learning and development.

Feedback is not about judgment—it's about learning. Every teacher, regardless of experience, has room to grow, and feedback serves as a guide to highlight what is working well and what can be improved. Constructive feedback should be viewed as a gift, not a punishment. When you approach it with an open mind, even the most challenging feedback can provide valuable insights that help refine your teaching techniques.

Great teachers are not born—they evolve. The most inspiring educators are those who continuously learn, adapt, and refine their methods. Every small adjustment you make based on feedback brings you closer to becoming the teacher your students need. By treating feedback as a mirror that reflects areas for growth, you unlock your full potential and create a more impactful and fulfilling teaching experience.

Feedback is all around you, waiting to be harnessed. The key is knowing where to find it and how to use it effectively. By tapping into multiple sources of feedback, you can refine your teaching strategies and enhance student learning outcomes. Three powerful sources of feedback that can elevate your teaching are student-centred feedback, peer and mentor feedback, and self-reflection tools.

Student-Centred Feedback: Student-centred feedback is one of the most valuable resources at your disposal. Your students' verbal and non-verbal responses—such as body language, engagement levels, and participation—offer direct insight into the effectiveness of your teaching methods. If students appear excited and engaged, your approach is likely working; if they seem confused or disinterested, adjustments may be necessary. Additionally, student work and performance on exams, assignments, and classroom activities provide tangible evidence of learning progress. Anonymous student reflections can also be insightful. Encouraging students to write about their learning experiences, using prompts like "One thing I wish my teacher knew...," can uncover valuable perspectives that may otherwise go unnoticed.

Peer and Mentor Feedback: Peer and mentor feedback provides an external viewpoint that can help you refine your teaching strategies. Inviting a trusted colleague to observe your class allows you to receive constructive criticism and fresh ideas. Insights from educational leaders, such as school administrators and mentors, offer a broader perspective on your instructional approach and classroom management. Engaging in co-teaching and collaborative lesson planning with other educators can further enhance your methods by exposing you to different teaching styles and strategies.

Self-reflection tools: Self-reflection tools allow you to assess your own teaching practices objectively. Recording and reviewing your lessons can reveal areas for improvement that may not be noticeable in the moment. Keeping a teaching journal, where you document daily experiences, challenges, and successes, enables you to identify recurring patterns and make necessary adjustments. By consistently engaging with these feedback sources, you can cultivate a growth mindset and continuously evolve as an educator.

Turning Feedback into Action

Receiving feedback is one thing; acting on it is another. The most effective teachers don't just listen to feedback—they use it to drive meaningful change. To truly grow as a teacher, it's essential to approach feedback with a strategic mindset and a commitment to continuous improvement.

The first step in using feedback effectively is to filter the noise. Not all feedback is equally valuable, so it's important to identify the insights that will have the greatest impact on your teaching. Constructive criticism from students, peers, and mentors should be prioritized over generic or unfounded remarks. By focusing on meaningful feedback, you can direct your energy toward areas that truly matter.

Next, create an action plan based on the feedback you receive. Setting SMART goals—Specific, Measurable, Achievable, Relevant, and Time-bound—helps turn vague suggestions into concrete steps. For instance, if students struggle with engagement, your action plan might include incorporating more interactive activities, such as group discussions or hands-on projects, over the next month. Having clear objectives makes it easier to track progress and ensure that the changes you implement are effective.

Finally, teaching is a dynamic process that requires continuous experimentation and refinement. Once you implement changes, assess their impact and make necessary adjustments. Not every new strategy will work perfectly on the first attempt, but by staying adaptable and open to iteration, you can fine-tune your approach over time.

The best teachers never stop growing. They embrace feedback not as a threat but as a tool for refinement. Every critique, suggestion, and observation is an opportunity to enhance your teaching practice and inspire your students. What's one piece of feedback you'll act on today? Commit to one small change, and watch how it transforms your classroom experience. Teaching is a journey, and every step forward brings you closer to mastery.

Chapter 22
Strengthening Parent Engagement

Strong parent engagement isn't just support—it's a partnership that empowers students, enriches learning, and builds a foundation for lifelong success.

A child's education does not exist in isolation. It is a dynamic and shared responsibility between you, the school administration, your students, and their parents. When these forces align, students experience greater academic success, emotional well-being, and personal growth. However, despite having the same end goal—the child's success—you and the parents often find yourselves at odds due to miscommunication, unmet expectations, or a lack of meaningful engagement. Strengthening parent involvement is not about formal meetings alone; it is about fostering a culture of collaboration, trust, and shared responsibility. By taking proactive steps, you can create an environment where parents feel valued as partners, rather than mere spectators, in their child's learning journey.

Moving Beyond the Traditional Parent-Teacher Meeting

For many parents, their primary interaction with you occurs during scheduled parent-teacher meetings, which typically focus on academic concerns or behavioural issues. While these formal discussions are important, they are often not enough to build a strong, ongoing partnership. If parents only hear from you when there is a problem, their perception of school communication may become negative or anxiety-inducing. Instead, strive for consistent, informal, and proactive communication.

Regular check-ins through emails, messaging apps, or digital learning platforms such as Google Classroom or ClassDojo can keep parents informed about classroom activities, student progress, and learning objectives. These updates do not need to be lengthy or overly detailed; even a brief message sharing a child's improvement, participation, or unique classroom contribution can strengthen the connection between home and school.

Additionally, you could well make an effort to highlight and celebrate small successes. Instead of reaching out only when there is a problem, share positive updates—such as improvements in effort, creativity, or collaboration—helping parents see their child's development beyond grades and test scores. When parents receive both positive and constructive feedback, they are more likely to engage in a supportive, rather than defensive, manner.

Creating a Culture of Mutual Respect

Parents care deeply about their children's success, but they may not always express their concerns in a way that aligns with school expectations. Stress, past experiences, and personal circumstances can influence how they communicate with you. In turn, you may feel unappreciated or misunderstood when parents challenge your teaching methods or question your decisions. The key to bridging this gap is to cultivate a culture of mutual respect through clear and empathetic communication.

Active listening plays a crucial role in this process. Before responding to a parent's concern, take a moment to acknowledge their feelings. A simple statement like, *"I understand that this is important to you, and I appreciate you bringing it to my attention,"* can defuse tension and build trust. Parents want to feel heard, and when you validate their concerns, they become more receptive to collaboration.

Moreover, be mindful of the language you use when communicating with parents. Avoiding complex educational jargon helps ensure that parents fully understand their child's progress and needs. For example, instead of saying, *"Your child needs to develop stronger metacognitive strategies for reading comprehension,"* a clearer approach would be, *"Your child is learning how to think about what they read and understand it better. We are working on strategies to improve this, and I'd love to share some ways you can support them at home."* When communication is accessible and relatable, parents feel more empowered to take an active role in their child's learning.

Turning Conflict into Collaboration

Not all interactions with parents will be smooth. Sometimes, differences in expectations, frustration, or misinformation can lead to challenging conversations. The key to handling these moments effectively is to remain calm, solution-focused, and open to finding common ground.

When faced with a difficult conversation, approach it with the mindset of collaboration rather than confrontation. Instead of responding defensively to criticism, acknowledge the parent's concern and steer the discussion toward constructive solutions. For example, if a parent expresses frustration about their child's grades, rather than saying, *"They need to study harder,"* try, *"I understand your concern. Let's explore some strategies that can help your child stay engaged and improve in this subject."*

Seeking common ground is essential in resolving conflicts. Even when parents and teachers see things differently, they can almost always agree on one thing: they both want what is best for the student. By keeping this shared goal at the centre of the conversation, educators can navigate difficult discussions with empathy and professionalism.

Building a True Partnership

A strong partnership between teachers and parents creates a powerful support system for students, reinforcing learning and personal development both at school and at home. However, this relationship requires ongoing effort, trust, and open communication. By establishing consistent and positive interactions, actively listening to parents' concerns, and focusing on collaboration rather than conflict, educators can transform parent engagement from a mere obligation into a meaningful and productive alliance.

What's one small way you can strengthen parent engagement today? Perhaps it's sending a quick message acknowledging a student's improvement, providing a simple learning tip for parents, or inviting parents to share their insights on their child's strengths and challenges. Even the smallest effort to engage parents can have a lasting impact, fostering a supportive community where students can truly thrive.

Cultural Sensitivity in Parent Engagement

As a teacher, you interact with parents from a variety of cultural backgrounds, each with unique values, beliefs, and expectations about education. Understanding these differences is essential in fostering positive and effective parent-teacher relationships. Some parents may emphasize academic excellence above all else, while others may prioritize holistic development, including emotional and social well-being. Being aware of these cultural perspectives helps you bridge potential gaps and create an inclusive environment where all families feel valued.

Language barriers can often hinder meaningful engagement between you and parents. To ensure clear communication, you can provide translated materials, collaborate with bilingual staff members, or use visual communication tools like infographics and videos. Additionally, hosting multilingual parent meetings or offering interpretation services can make non-native speakers feel more included. Your goal is to empower all parents to participate in their child's education, regardless of their language proficiency.

Respecting different parental expectations is crucial for building trust. While some parents may prefer direct involvement in academic decisions, others may take a more hands-off approach due to cultural norms or work commitments. Instead of using a one-size-fits-all approach, you can offer multiple ways for parents to stay involved, such as informal discussions, workshops, or volunteering opportunities. A culturally responsive approach fosters stronger connections between you, parents, and students, ultimately benefiting everyone.

Leveraging Technology for Better Communication

Technology has transformed the way you communicate with parents, offering more transparency and accessibility than ever before. Digital platforms such as Google Classroom, ClassDojo, or school apps enable you to share updates, progress reports, and resources instantly, keeping parents informed and engaged. These tools also allow for two-way communication, where parents can ask questions, share concerns, or provide feedback without needing to schedule in-person meetings.

However, while digital communication has many benefits, it is important to establish clear boundaries to maintain a healthy work-life balance. You should set expectations regarding response times to messages and emails, ensuring that communication remains professional and manageable. Encouraging structured interactions, such as designated parent-teacher chat hours, can help you prevent burnout while still fostering meaningful engagement.

Beyond school updates, technology can also support home-based learning. You can guide parents on how to use educational apps, interactive websites, and online learning resources to reinforce classroom instruction. Offering workshops or tutorial sessions can help parents become comfortable with these tools, ensuring that technology serves as a bridge rather than a barrier in the learning process.

Encouraging Parent Involvement Beyond Academics

Parental involvement should extend beyond test scores and homework. When parents engage in broader school activities, your students benefit from a well-rounded support system that nurtures their academic, social, and emotional growth. You can invite parents to contribute in meaningful ways, such as volunteering in classroom observation, serving as mentors, or sharing their professional expertise through career talks. This not only enhances your students' learning experiences but also strengthens the sense of community within your school.

Creating collaborative learning experiences at home and school fosters deeper engagement. You can organize family-oriented activities such as reading challenges, STEM projects, or art exhibitions where parents and children work together. These initiatives encourage parents to take an active role in their child's education in a non-pressured, enjoyable way, reinforcing the idea that learning is a shared journey.

An inclusive environment ensures that all parents feel welcome and comfortable participating, regardless of their background or schedule constraints. Providing flexible engagement opportunities, such as virtual parent meetings and weekend events allows more parents to take part without feeling overwhelmed. The more you make parents feel included and valued, the more likely they are to support and engage with their child's educational journey.

Supporting Parents in Their Role as Educators

Many parents want to support their child's learning at home but may feel unsure of how to do so effectively. You can provide simple, practical strategies that empower them to reinforce classroom learning without feeling overwhelmed. Sharing small, manageable learning activities—such as daily reading habits, engaging math games, or discussion prompts—allows parents to integrate learning into their routines. Even 10–15 minutes of focused learning at home can make a significant impact on your students' progress.

Helping parents understand child development stages is key to setting realistic expectations. Some parents may become frustrated if their child struggles with certain subjects or developmental milestones. By guiding them on what is developmentally appropriate for different age groups and suggesting tailored approaches, you can help them provide more effective and patient support. When parents have the right knowledge, they can work alongside you to help their children succeed.

Additionally, it's important to acknowledge the stress that comes with parenting and offer tips for maintaining a positive learning environment at home. You can suggest simple strategies such as setting up a distraction-free study space, establishing consistent routines, and encouraging open-ended conversations about school. When parents feel supported in their role, they are more likely to engage actively and confidently in their child's education—making your job as a teacher even more effective.

Handling Difficult Parents and Resistance to Engagement

Not all parents engage in the same way, and some may appear disinterested or even resistant to involvement. This disengagement can stem from various reasons, including negative past school experiences, time constraints, or feelings of intimidation. Instead of assuming disinterest, you can take proactive steps to understand the root cause and find personalized ways to encourage participation. A non-judgmental and open-minded approach can make a significant difference in re-engaging hesitant parents.

Difficult conversations with confrontational or overly demanding parents can be challenging, but they must be handled with patience and professionalism. When faced with criticism or complaints, it is important to remain calm and acknowledge the parent's concerns without becoming defensive. Using active listening strategies—such as repeating back concerns *"I understand that you're worried about your child's progress, and you feel that more individual attention is needed."*, asking clarifying questions *"Could you help me understand what specific challenges your child is facing in the subject?"*, and proposing collaborative solutions *"Let's work together to find ways to support your child both at school and at home. Perhaps we can set up a regular progress check-in."*—can help you de-escalate tension and foster a more productive dialogue.

Balancing school policies with individual parental concerns is another key challenge. While you must adhere to institutional guidelines, you should also remain flexible in addressing unique family needs. Offering alternative solutions or accommodations where possible can help build trust and cooperation. Ultimately, a strong and respectful parent-teacher relationship, even in challenging situations, ensures the best outcomes for your students.

Chapter 23
Maximising Impact Through Time Management

Time is a teacher's greatest tool—manage it wisely...

As a teacher, you often feel like there aren't enough hours in the day. Your to-do list grows faster than you can check items off. Between lesson planning, grading, meetings, and responding to student needs, it may seem like time is slipping through your fingers. But what if you could take control of your time rather than letting it control you?

Mastering time management is not about squeezing more tasks into your day; it's about making intentional choices that allow you to focus on what truly matters—impacting your students' learning and growth while maintaining your own well-being. In this chapter, you will learn how to work smarter, not harder, and create a balanced approach to time management that enhances both your effectiveness and personal satisfaction.

Identifying Time Vampires

Before you can take control of your time, you need to understand where it's going. Many teachers unknowingly lose valuable hours to non-essential tasks, leaving them exhausted and with little energy for what truly matters—teaching and inspiring students. Time vampires silently drain productivity, making the workday feel longer and less effective.

Some of the biggest time drains include excessive paperwork, endless administrative tasks, and responding to unnecessary to-do lists of the day. Unstructured lesson planning can eat up hours, especially when searching for resources without a clear system. Frequent interruptions—like impromptu meetings, constant emails, and minor classroom disruptions—further chip away at focus and efficiency. Even grading can become a time trap when done without streamlined strategies. Additionally, disorganized classroom routines lead to wasted minutes during transitions, reducing instructional time.

The first step to reclaiming your time is identifying these drains. Try keeping a Time Journal for a week, documenting your daily activities and how long they take. At the end of the week, you may be surprised by where your time is slipping away. This awareness is the foundation for smarter time management—allowing you to work more efficiently, enhance student learning, and maintain your well-being.

Time management isn't about doing more—it's about doing what truly matters. By making intentional choices, you can streamline your workload, boost productivity, and create more space for meaningful teaching and personal well-being. Following are the few strategies for effective time management:

Pareto Principle (80/20 rule): One of the most powerful strategies is the Pareto Principle (80/20 rule), which suggests that 20% of your efforts yield 80% of your results. Rather than striving for perfection in every task, identify high-impact activities and prioritize them. For example, instead of spending excessive time on classroom decorations, shift your energy toward student-centered learning strategies that enhance engagement and comprehension. By focusing on what truly makes a difference, you can achieve better outcomes with less stress.

Eisenhower Matrix: Prioritization is key, and the Eisenhower Matrix helps categorize tasks based on urgency and importance:

- ✓ Urgent & Important: Lesson delivery, student emergencies, urgent parent communications—handle these immediately.

- ✓ Important but Not Urgent: Professional development, refining teaching strategies—schedule these proactively.

- ✓ Urgent but Less Important: Routine administrative tasks, non-essential emails—delegate when possible.

- ✓ Neither Urgent nor Important: Excessive social media scrolling, redundant paperwork—eliminate these.

Batching Tasks: Another effective time-saving strategy is batching similar tasks together. Instead of constantly shifting between different activities, which can waste time and mental energy, group related tasks into dedicated time blocks. For example, set aside specific grading sessions rather than marking papers randomly throughout the day. Plan an entire week's worth of lessons in one sitting instead of preparing them on a daily basis. Similarly, schedule designated times for responding to emails rather than checking them continuously. By minimizing context switching, you can work more efficiently and maintain better focus throughout your day. These strategies not only help you take control of your time but also allow you to work smarter, reducing stress while enhancing your effectiveness in the classroom. By making small but intentional changes, you can create a more balanced and fulfilling teaching experience.

Automating and delegating: Automating and delegating can also significantly reduce your workload. You don't have to do everything alone—some tasks can be automated using digital tools like Google Forms, Kahoot, or online grading systems, while others can be shared with students or colleagues. Structured peer-learning activities allow students to review each other's work using clear rubrics, while well-structured classroom routines help students transition smoothly between activities, reducing disruptions. Creating reusable templates for lesson plans, emails, and worksheets saves valuable time and effort.

Setting Boundaries: Finally, setting boundaries is crucial for protecting your time and energy. Learning to say no to unnecessary commitments ensures that your focus remains on what truly matters. Establishing "focus hours"—such as turning off notifications while grading or lesson planning—minimizes distractions and boosts productivity. Most importantly, prioritizing self-care is not a luxury but a necessity. A well-rested, mentally refreshed teacher is more effective, engaged, and inspiring in the classroom. When you take care of yourself, your students benefit too. By making small yet intentional changes, you can work smarter, not harder—creating a balanced, fulfilling, and impactful teaching experience.

Own Your Time, Own Your Impact

The most successful teachers don't simply react to their workload; they take a proactive approach to planning, ensuring they stay in control rather than feeling overwhelmed. If you want to manage your time effectively, reduce stress, and focus on what truly matters—your students' learning—you need to plan ahead. Establishing a structured weekly planning routine can set the tone for a productive and balanced week. On Sunday evening or Monday morning, take a few moments to set clear goals for the week. Block out time specifically for lesson preparation, grading, and student support so that you don't find yourself rushing at the last minute. Identifying potential obstacles in advance and creating backup plans can also help you navigate unexpected challenges without derailing your progress.

Daily prioritization is just as important as weekly planning. Start each day by identifying your top three priorities so that you remain focused on what truly matters. Using a planner or digital tool can help you stay organized and ensure that nothing slips through the cracks. At the end of the day, take a few minutes to reflect on what worked well and what needs adjustment. This simple habit will allow you to continuously refine your time management strategies and become more efficient. By consistently planning ahead and prioritizing effectively, you can create a structured and fulfilling work routine, allowing you to be more present and engaged in your teaching while maintaining a healthier work-life balance.

Time is your most valuable resource, and when you learn to manage it effectively, you gain clarity, reduce stress, and maximize your impact in the classroom. By taking control of your time, you can be more present for your students, bring your best self to teaching, and still have energy left for your personal life. Instead of feeling overwhelmed by endless tasks, a strategic approach to time management helps you focus on what truly matters—engaging with your students, fostering meaningful learning experiences, and maintaining a sense of balance in your daily routine.

Small changes can lead to significant improvements. Consider one habit you can change today that will help you save time and increase your impact. Whether it's setting clearer priorities, streamlining repetitive tasks, or establishing firm boundaries, every step toward better time management empowers you to teach more effectively while maintaining your well-being. When you own your time, you take charge of your professional and personal life, ensuring that both are fulfilling and sustainable.

Chapter 24
Managing Career and Finances

Financial literacy is essential for teachers—not just to manage earnings but to create stability, reduce stress, and build a future where passion and security go hand in hand.

Financial literacy is a crucial but often overlooked aspect of a teacher's professional life. While teachers dedicate their careers to shaping young minds, many struggle with financial instability due to a lack of formal financial education. Teaching is a profession driven by passion, but financial stress can significantly impact a teacher's job satisfaction, mental well-being, and overall quality of life. Many teachers find themselves living pay check to pay check, burdened by loans, household expenses, and unpredictable salary structures. Without proper financial planning, retirement may seem uncertain, and day-to-day expenses may become overwhelming.

As a teacher, you dedicate your life to shaping young minds, inspiring growth, and making a difference in the world. However, while teaching is a calling fuelled by passion, financial well-being is equally important. A secure and well-managed financial life allows you to focus on your mission without the stress of economic uncertainty. But here's the good news—you have the power to take control of your financial future. With the right knowledge and strategies, you can achieve financial stability, reduce stress, and create a secure foundation for yourself and your family.

Teaching is often described as a noble profession, but nobility alone doesn't pay the bills. While you may not have the highest pay check compared to other professions, you do have access to financial opportunities that can enhance your quality of life. By taking proactive steps today—whether it's creating a budget, leveraging financial benefits, or investing in lifelong learning—you set yourself on a path toward financial freedom. When you feel secure, confident, and valued, you bring your best self to the classroom. And when teachers prosper, the entire education system benefits. Your financial well-being is not just about you—it's about sustaining the passion that makes you a great educator. So, take charge of your finances, and continue inspiring the next generation with confidence and peace of mind.

Teaching with Financial Confidence

Financial security is essential for a fulfilling teaching career. When teachers are not burdened by financial worries, they can focus more on their students, creativity, and personal well-being. Small but consistent financial planning can lead to long-term stability. Here are a few steps you can take to ensure financial confidence:

- ✓ Understand your health benefits and insurance coverage to avoid unexpected medical expenses.

- ✓ Track and claim tax deductions for education-related expenses, ensuring that you keep more of your salary.

- ✓ Invest in continuous learning and professional development to enhance career prospects and financial growth.

- ✓ Review your pension or provident fund contributions and make necessary adjustments for a secure retirement.

By taking control of your financial situation today, you can teach with confidence, live with peace of mind, and build a future that is both secure and rewarding.

Managing money effectively is essential for teachers, especially since many faces inconsistent pay structures, unpaid vacation periods, and rising living expenses. A well-structured financial plan helps educators maintain stability and avoid financial hardship. One of the best ways to achieve this is through budgeting.

A zero-based budget is a highly effective budgeting method where every single income is assigned to a specific category—expenses, savings, or investments—so that income minus expenses equals zero. This strategy ensures that all funds are used wisely, preventing unnecessary spending and encouraging intentional saving. Teachers should categorize their budget into fixed expenses (such as rent or mortgage payments), variable expenses (such as groceries and transportation), debt repayments, and savings. By tracking their spending habits and making necessary adjustments, teachers can create a sustainable financial plan that supports both their immediate and long-term needs.

Another challenge many teachers face is managing income during school vacation months. Taking on seasonal or freelance work—such as tutoring, online teaching, or educational consulting—can help supplement income during breaks. Additionally, proactive financial planning and building an emergency fund ensure stability even during non-teaching periods.

Diversifying Income Sources for Greater Financial Security

While teaching salaries provide a stable income, diversifying earnings can significantly improve financial security and create additional opportunities for wealth-building. Many teachers have valuable skills that can be monetized outside the classroom, helping them earn extra income while maintaining their passion for education.

One of the most accessible ways to supplement income is private tutoring. Offering one-on-one tutoring sessions, either in person or online, can be a lucrative side job. Many students and parents seek additional academic support, and teachers can leverage their expertise to provide valuable educational services. Similarly, coaching extracurricular activities, such as sports, music, or drama, can bring in additional earnings.

Teachers with strong communication skills can also explore consulting and workshop facilitation. Conducting professional development sessions for fellow educators, assisting with curriculum design, or creating educational content for publishers can open new financial opportunities. Additionally, writing and content creation can be a sustainable passive income stream. Teachers can write educational blogs, publish books, or create online courses that generate ongoing revenue.

For those looking to build long-term wealth, investing can be a powerful tool. Investing in stocks, mutual funds, real estate, or low-maintenance business ventures can provide passive income and financial security. Teachers should explore different investment options and seek financial advice to create a diversified portfolio that aligns with their financial goals. By expanding income streams beyond their salaries, teachers can gain greater financial independence and reduce reliance on a single pay-check.

Avoiding Debt Traps and Planning for Long-Term Financial Security

Many teachers face financial challenges, whether from personal loans, home mortgages, auto loans, credit cards, or everyday expenses. While taking on debt is sometimes necessary, managing it wisely is essential to ensuring long-term financial well-being. Developing smart financial strategies can help educators navigate their obligations effectively and avoid common financial pitfalls.

One important strategy is prioritizing the repayment of high-interest debt. Credit card balances and high-interest loans can accumulate quickly, leading to financial strain. Teachers can benefit from focusing on paying off these debts first while maintaining minimum payments on lower-interest obligations. Setting up automated payments can also help ensure timely payments, preventing late fees and protecting credit scores.

Maintaining a strong credit score is equally important, as it impacts future financial opportunities such as homeownership, loan approvals, and favorable interest rates. Responsible credit use—such as keeping balances low, making timely payments, and avoiding unnecessary borrowing—can contribute to long-term financial stability. Additionally, adopting mindful spending habits and focusing on savings can prevent financial challenges down the road.

Building an emergency fund is another crucial step toward financial security. Setting aside three to six months' worth of living expenses provides a safety net in case of unexpected situations such as medical emergencies, job transitions, or urgent home repairs. In addition to short-term savings, retirement planning should be a priority. Maximizing contributions to pension plans, exploring investment options, and beginning the savings journey early can ensure a comfortable and secure future. The earlier teachers start preparing for retirement, the more financially independent they will be when they choose to step away from the classroom.

Financial literacy is an empowering tool that allows teachers to take control of their financial well-being, reduce stress, and remain focused on their passion for teaching. By understanding their total compensation, adopting smart budgeting techniques, managing debt effectively, and diversifying income sources, educators can build a strong financial foundation.

Rather than viewing financial management as a burden, teachers can embrace it as an opportunity to create a fulfilling and worry-free life. With the right financial habits, educators can achieve greater financial freedom, reduce uncertainty, and look forward to a secure future. Every small financial decision made today contributes to long-term stability and peace of mind.

What is one financial habit you can improve today? Whether it's starting a savings plan, paying down debt, or exploring additional income sources, taking one proactive step can make a meaningful difference in achieving financial security.

Chapter 25
The Day You Retire

Retirement isn't the end—it's a celebration of every lesson taught, every life inspired, and every difference made. Your impact lives on, and a new journey begins!

One day, the bell will ring for the last time, and you will step out of the classroom, no longer as a teacher but as a traveller stepping into a new chapter of life.

The desk where you once sat, reviewing assignments and offering words of encouragement, will belong to someone else. The chalkboard or whiteboard where you explained complex concepts and scribbled formulas will be erased, making room for new lessons. The students who filled your classroom with laughter, curiosity, and questions will move forward, carrying pieces of you with them.

It is a day every teacher knows will come, yet when it arrives, it feels surreal. Because teaching was never just a job—it was a calling, a journey of shaping minds, building dreams, and nurturing souls. And now, that journey shifts from leading a classroom to watching the seeds you planted bloom in the world.

You will no longer have to wake up early to prepare for a day of teaching. No more lesson plans, no more report cards, no more teachers' meetings. The final school bell will ring, and for the first time in years—perhaps decades—you will step out of the school building, not as a teacher with tomorrow's tasks in mind, but as someone stepping into the unknown.

There will be a flood of emotions—relief, nostalgia, uncertainty, joy, and perhaps even a touch of sadness. Because, for so long, your identity has been tied to the classroom. And now, you wonder: *Who am I, if not a teacher?*

The Footprints Left Behind

Teaching was never just about the curriculum. It was about nurturing minds, shaping dreams, and planting seeds of knowledge that would grow long after your time in the classroom.

Long after you've stepped away, your influence will continue to ripple through generations. The child you once consoled after they failed a test may now be a confident adult navigating life with resilience because of the encouragement you gave them. The student who struggled with math but kept trying because of your patience might one day teach their own child with the same kindness.

Your classroom was never just a space for learning—it was a place where futures were built, where young hearts found encouragement, and where knowledge became a bridge to endless possibilities. And that does not disappear the day you retire.

Retirement is a transition, not a farewell. The beauty of teaching is that your words, your presence, and your impact do not fade. They live on in the lives of your students, shaping the future in ways you may never fully witness.

Perhaps you will see it in a former student who returns years later, just to say, *"Thank you, Teacher. You changed my life."* Or maybe you will hear it in an unexpected message: *"I never told you this, Teacher, but you were the reason I didn't give up."*

Sometimes, the impact will remain unseen, quietly unfolding in the lives of those who once sat in your classroom, who now carry forward the lessons you taught—not just the subjects but the lessons of life, courage, kindness, and perseverance.

As you step into this new chapter, take a moment to reflect on the journey that brought you here.

Think back to the first time you stood in front of a class. The nervousness, the uncertainty, the overwhelming feeling of responsibility. You wondered if you would ever get it right. Over time, you found your rhythm. You learned how to read the expressions of students—when they were engaged, when they were struggling, and when they needed an extra push. You discovered that teaching was as much about understanding human nature as it was about delivering lessons. **And as the years passed, you didn't just teach; you mentored. You guided. You inspired.**

There were difficult days—the students who refused to listen, the moments of frustration, the endless hours of grading. There were times when you questioned whether your efforts even made a difference. But you kept going. Because you believed that every student, no matter how difficult, deserved a chance. You learned to adapt, to innovate, to find ways to reach even the most reluctant learner. **And in doing so, you didn't just shape your students—you grew as well.**

Some of the greatest rewards of teaching were never in the salary or accolades. They were in the small, quiet moments:

✓ The look of triumph on a student's face when they finally understood something they had struggled with.

✓ The student who once doubted themselves but went on to achieve great things.

✓ The ones who left your class not just with knowledge, but with a sense of confidence and belief in themselves.

Teaching was never just about imparting facts. It was about changing lives.

New Journey

Stepping away from the classroom does not mean stepping away from your purpose. Your role as an educator simply takes on a new form. The lessons you have shared, the encouragement you have given, and the lives you have influenced will continue to ripple through generations. Teaching was never just about the subject matter; it was about shaping minds, nurturing confidence, and igniting curiosity. Even as you close this chapter, your story as a teacher is far from over—it is merely evolving.

Retirement opens new doors, offering a chance to guide others in different ways. Now, you have the wisdom and experience to mentor new teachers, helping them navigate the same challenges you once faced. Your insights can shape the future of education, not through lesson plans and lectures, but through conversations, mentorship, and sharing your journey. The knowledge you carry is invaluable, and by passing it on, you continue to build a legacy beyond the walls of any classroom.

Beyond mentorship, retirement is an opportunity to document the incredible moments of your teaching career. Every teacher has a wealth of experiences—stories of struggles and triumphs, of students who left lasting impressions, of moments that defined their career. Now, with time on your side, you can write these memories down, whether in a book, a blog, or personal reflections. Your words can serve as a source of inspiration for future educators and students alike. By sharing your experiences, you ensure that the lessons learned in your classroom live on in ways you may never have imagined.

Yet, teaching was never just about giving knowledge—it was also about learning. Retirement is not the end of learning; rather, it is a new beginning. Now is the time to explore subjects you always wished you had time for. Read widely, travel to places that have long fascinated you, pick up hobbies that spark your curiosity. Because a great teacher never stops learning, and even in retirement, the thirst for knowledge remains an integral part of who you are.

Beyond personal growth, you may also find fulfillment in giving back to your community in new ways. Perhaps you will discover joy in volunteering, in community service, in supporting young learners outside the school system. The classroom may be behind you, but the heart of a teacher never fades. Your expertise and passion can still make a difference, whether by tutoring a struggling student, helping an underprivileged school, or lending your voice to educational causes. The world still needs your wisdom, your patience, and your kindness.

Retirement is not the end of your story—it is simply a new chapter, one filled with different lessons and new opportunities. As you reflect on your journey, celebrate the challenges you overcame, the lives you touched, and the knowledge you imparted. The work of a teacher is never truly finished, and even as you step away from the classroom, your impact continues to shape the future. You may no longer stand before a class, but your influence will live on in the minds and hearts of those you once taught. That is the true legacy of a teacher.

Once a Teacher, Always a Teacher-Your Legacy Lives On

What is a teacher's legacy? It is not found in retirement plaques or farewell speeches. It is not in years of service or academic achievements. Your true legacy is found in the lives you have touched. It is in the student who once feared failure but now stands strong. It is in the quiet ones who found their voice, in the restless ones who learned patience, and in the struggling ones who discovered their strength—all because of you.

Your name may fade from the school records, but your influence will not. Long after your final lesson, your words, your encouragement, and your belief in your students will continue to shape their journeys. The knowledge you imparted, the confidence you instilled, and the values you nurtured will live on in the choices they make and the lives they lead. That is the true measure of a teacher's impact—not in what is written in history, but in what is carried forward in hearts and minds.

Even as you retire, the heart of a teacher never fades. You will still find yourself giving advice, encouraging young minds, and offering wisdom in unexpected places. Teaching is not just a career—it is a calling, a lifelong mission that does not end when you step out of the classroom. You will see lessons in everyday moments, find opportunities to uplift others, and continue shaping the world in ways both big and small.

So, walk into this new chapter with your head held high, knowing that your work is not over—it has simply transformed. Whether through mentorship or acts of kindness, your influence will continue to inspire. You were, are, and always will be a teacher. And that is a legacy beyond the classroom.

Once a Teacher, Always a Teacher

The bell may ring its final chime,

Marking the end of classroom time.

The lessons taught, the books set down,

Yet still, you wear the teacher's crown.

No longer bound by schoolyard walls,

Yet wisdom answers when it calls.

The hands that guided, shaped, and raised,

Still spark the minds they once amazed.

The echoes of your gentle voice,

Still teach of kindness, strength, and choice.

In every heart where dreams take flight,

Your lessons glow, a guiding light.

No chalk in hand, no desk in sight,

Yet still, you shine—a beacon bright.

For teaching is not bound by years,

It lives beyond, through love and tears.

So though you leave the classroom door,

Your journey teaches evermore.

For once a teacher, this is true,

The world still learns because of you.

* * *

Concluding Note

Dear Teacher,

As you turn this final page, I hope this journey of reflection, growth, and discovery has resonated with you. Teaching is not just about delivering lessons—it is about shaping lives, including your own. Through this book, we have explored self-mastery, the science of learning, innovative teaching strategies, and professional growth. But beyond all these, one truth stands firm: **a great teacher is first a great learner.**

You have the power to transform not just your students but also yourself. Every challenge you face in the classroom is an opportunity to grow. Every lesson you teach is a chance to inspire. Every student you guide is a story in the making. Your impact goes beyond textbooks and lesson plans—it is felt in the minds you nurture, the confidence you instil, and the futures you help shape.

As you move forward, remember that teaching is not about achieving perfection but about embracing progress. Keep questioning, keep experimenting, and most importantly, keep learning. Your willingness to evolve will not only make you a better educator but also a lifelong inspiration to those you teach.

Thank you for dedicating your life to education. The world needs passionate, reflective, and ever-learning teachers like you. May your journey ahead be filled with curiosity, courage, and the enduring joy of learning.

May the inner teacher in you be awakened, guiding you to inspire generations to come.